HOW WRITING
CAME ABOUT

P9-AQU-796

How Writing Came About

DENISE SCHMANDT-BESSERAT

University of Texas Press
Austin

Abridged edition of *Before Writing, Volume I: From Counting to Cuneiform*

Copyright © 1992, 1996 by the University of Texas Press
All rights reserved
Printed in the United States of America

First abridged edition, 1996

Requests for permission to reproduce material from this work should be sent to Permissions, University of Texas Press, Box 7819, Austin, TX 78713-7819.

♾The paper used in this publication meets the minimum requirements of American National Standard for Information Sciences — Permanence of Paper for Printed Library Materials, ANSI Z39.48-1984.

LIBRARY OF CONGRESS CATALOGING IN PUBLICATION DATA

Schmandt-Besserat, Denise.
    How writing came about / Denise Schmandt-Besserat.— 1st abridged ed.
      p.   cm.
    "Abridged edition of Before Writing, Volume I: From Counting to Cuneiform."
    Includes index.
    ISBN 0-292-77704-3 (pbk. : alk. paper)
    1. Tokens — Middle East.   2. Writing — History.   3. Middle East —
Antiquities.   I. Schmandt-Besserat, Denise. Before writing.   II. Title.
CJ4867.S364   1996
737'.3'0956 — dc20   95-41829

To our three grandchildren, who give us such great joy: **NICOLAUS**

DANIELLE

MICHAEL

Contents

Preface

THIS BOOK IS AN ABRIDGED version of *Before Writing*, published in 1992 by the University of Texas Press. That work was issued in two volumes — *I: From Counting to Cuneiform* and *II: A Catalog of Near Eastern Tokens* — and was addressed primarily to specialists. The purpose of the present abridgment is to offer the general reader a less detailed and more affordable book. I have made no changes in this volume except for variations in editing, minor corrections, and updating a few references.

How Writing Came About constitutes the first comprehensive study of Near Eastern tokens to be aimed at a general audience. Based on the analysis and interpretation of a selection of eight thousand specimens from 116 sites in Iran, Iraq, the Levant, and Turkey, it documents the immediate precursor of the cuneiform script, the world's first writing system. The material, dating from 8000 to 3000 B.C. and mostly unpublished before, was collected and studied firsthand in thirty museums in fifteen countries. Also included here is my systematic study of the 200 envelopes, used to keep tokens in archives, and the 240 impressed tablets now known. These two types of objects illustrate the major steps in the transition from tokens to writing.

The tokens from early excavations often lack a precise stratigraphy. Even so, the large assemblage presented here gives a reliable picture of the types and subtypes of the counters, their geographic and chronological distribution, their evolution over time, and the transition from tokens to writing. This book is organized into three parts, as follows.

PART ONE: THE EVIDENCE

The first two chapters are devoted to the documentation of the archaeological material. Chapter 1 describes the counters, their shapes, markings, and manufacture, and their evolution from "plain" to "complex" tokens. Chapter 2 identifies the context in which the tokens were used: the type of settlements to which they belonged; their spacial distribution within those settlements; the structures and assemblages with which they were associated. Special attention is given to the rare tokens found in tombs.

Chapter 3 describes the fourth-millennium methods for holding tokens in archives — in particular, the envelopes. The following topics are covered: discovery of the envelopes, their number, geographic distribution, chronology, and context, the assemblages of tokens they held, the markings they bore, and their role in the transmutation of tokens into writing.

Chapter 4 deals with impressed tablets. After a review of the history of their discovery, their number, geographic distribution, chronology, and context, the documents and the signs they bear are described and their contribution to writing is assessed.

PART TWO: THE INTERPRETATION

The last three chapters analyze the role of tokens in the evolution of communication, social structures, and cognitive skills. These interpretations are tentative. There is no doubt that some of the conclusions will have to be revised in the future, when more and better data will be available.

In Chapter 5, tokens are interpreted as the second step in the development of record keeping, following Paleolithic tallies. The token was the first code to record economic data, providing the immediate background for the invention of writing.

Chapter 6 shows how the economy determined the token system and how, in turn, the counters had an impact on society.

Chapter 7 discusses the evolution of counting and its role in the invention of writing. Tokens are shown to reflect an archaic mode of "concrete counting," while writing derived from abstract counting.

In the Conclusions, I summarize the wealth of information provided by tokens on communication, mathematics, economy, social structures, and cognitive skills in prehistoric Near Eastern cultures.

PART THREE: THE ARTIFACTS

The charts in Part Three provide a graphic representation of the sixteen types of tokens and their subtypes. For more information, the reader is invited to consult the complete listing of tokens and the photographic documentation in *Before Writing, Volume II: A Catalog of Near Eastern Tokens.*

HOW WRITING
CAME ABOUT

Tokens, a New Theory

Man's development and the growth of civilizations have depended, in the main, on progress in a few activities — the discovery of fire, domestication of animals, the division of labor; but, above all, in the evolution of means to receive, to communicate, and to record his knowledge, and especially in the development of phonetic writing.
— COLIN CHERRY [1]

SPEECH, THE UNIVERSAL WAY by which humans communicate and transmit experience, fades instantly: before a word is fully pronounced it has already vanished forever. Writing, the first technology to make the spoken word permanent, changed the human condition.

It was a revolution in communication when a script allowed individuals to share information without meeting face to face. Writing also made it possible to store information, creating a pool of knowledge well beyond the ability of any single human to master yet, at the same time, available to all. Writing is regarded as the threshold of history, because it ended the reliance upon oral tradition, with all the inaccuracies this entailed. Business and administration are now inconceivable without bookkeeping to balance income and expenditures. Finally, among the innumerable benefits created by a script, writing allows us to capture our ideas when they arise and, in time, to sort and scrutinize, revise, add, subtract, and rectify them to arrive at a rigor of logic and a depth of thought that would otherwise be impossible.

How did writing come about? It is now generally agreed that writing was invented in Mesopotamia, present-day Iraq, in the late fourth millennium B.C.[2] and spread from there to Egypt, Elam, and the Indus Valley.[3] It is also generally agreed that other scripts developed later, independently, in China and Mesoamerica.[4] The origin of Chinese and Mesoamerican writing is still enigmatic. In this book, I will present the archaeological evidence that the Mesopotamian script derived from an archaic counting device. This immediate precursor of the cuneiform script was a system of tokens — small clay counters of many shapes which served for counting and accounting for goods in the prehistoric cultures of the Near East. The idea that Mesopotamian writing emerged from a counting device is new. Until the eighteenth century, the origin of writing was the subject of myths crediting gods, fabulous creatures, or heroes for its invention. Then, in the Age of Enlightenment, the theory that scripts started with picture writing was put forward. This view endured until the present.[5] In the following pages, I will show how the conception of the origin of writing evolved through time.

THE MYTHS

The oldest account of the invention of writing is perhaps that of the Sumerian epic *Enmerkar and the Lord of Aratta*.[6] The poem relates how Enmerkar, the lord of Uruk-Kulaba, sent an emissary to the lord of Aratta soliciting timber, gold, silver, lapis lazuli, and precious stones to rebuild the residence of the goddess Inanna. Back and forth the messenger delivered word for word the pleas, threats, and challenges between the two lords, until the day Enmerkar's instructions were too difficult for the emissary to memorize. The lord of Kulaba promptly invented writing, tracing his message on a clay tablet:

> —The emissary, his mouth (being) heavy, was not able to repeat (it).
> —Because the emissary, his mouth (being) heavy, was not able to repeat (it),
> —The lord of Kulaba patted clay and wrote the message like (on a present-day) tablet—
> —Formerly, the writing of messages on clay was not established—
> —Now, with Utu's bringing forth the day, verily this was so,
> —The lord of Kulaba inscribed the message like (on a present-day) tablet, this, verily, was so.[7]

One might add here that, according to the Sumerian king list, Enmerkar lived about 2700 B.C., when writing had been a common practice for five hundred years. Of course this casts doubts on the actual contribution of Enmerkar to the invention of writing!

In a second Sumerian poem, *Inanna and Enki, the Transfer of the Arts of Civilization from Eridu to Erech*, writing is conceived as one of a hundred basic elements of civilization held by Enki, the lord of wisdom.[8] Inanna coveted the divine decrees for her city, Uruk, and set her mind to getting them. This was done when Enki, drunk, donated to her each and every one of the crafts. In Samuel Noah Kramer's words:

> After their hearts had become happy with drinks, Enki exclaims: . . .
>   " . . . O name of my power, O name of my power,
> To the bright Inanna, my daughter, I shall present . . .
> The arts of woodworking, metalworking, writing, toolmaking,
> leatherworking, . . . building, basketweaving."
> Pure Inanna took them.[9]

Inanna loaded writing and the other divine decrees onto the Boat of Heaven and started an eventful journey back to Uruk. After overcoming tempests and sea monsters, sent by Enki to recapture his possessions, she finally reached the city, where she unloaded her precious booty to the delight of her people.

According to Berossus' *Babyloniaca*, Oannes, a sea creature with the body of a fish and the head, feet, and voice of a man, gave to the Babylonians the knowledge of writing, language, science, and crafts of all types.[10] In other Babylonian texts, the god Ea, the lord of wisdom, was the source of all secret magical knowledge, writing in particular.[11] In Assyria, Nabu, son of Marduk, was revered as the instructor of mankind in all arts and crafts, including building, agriculture, and writing.[12]

In the Bible, God revealed his will to mankind with the Tables of the Law "written by the finger of God."[13] The source of great debates,[14] these words were interpreted by Daniel Defoe as meaning that "the two Tables, written by the Finger of God in Mount *Sinai*, was the first Writing in the World; and that all other Alphabets derive from the *Hebrew*"(fig. 1).[15] Oth-

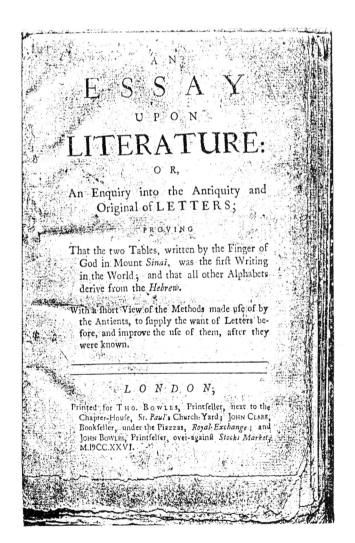

Fig. 1. Title page of Daniel Defoe's *An Essay upon Literature* (London: Thomas Bowles, 1726). Courtesy Harry Ransom Humanities Research Center, University of Texas at Austin.

ers credited Adam as the inventor of writing. In 1668, John Wilkins, one of the founders of the Royal Society and an influential and respected English scholar,[16] commented that Adam had invented the Hebrew alphabet: "though not immediately after his creation, yet in process of time, upon his experience of their great necessity and usefulness."[17]

The myths, from Sumer to Daniel Defoe, share one common characteristic: they present writing as emerging, on one day, as a full-fledged script. None of them conveys the notion of an evolution from a simple to a more complex system of communication. The concept of a ready-made alphabet handed down from heaven persisted until the eighteenth century.

THE PICTOGRAPHIC THEORY

In the eighteenth century, William Warburton, bishop of Gloucester, introduced the first evolutionary theory of writing. Based on his observations of Egyptian, Chinese, and Aztec manuscripts, Warburton argued that all scripts originally developed from narrative drawings. In time, he said, these pictures became more and more simplified and developed into abstract characters. The theory was presented in Warburton's book, *Divine Legation of Moses*, published in London in 1738.[18] The ideas made their way into Diderot and d'Alembert's *Encyclopédie*, in the article entitled "Ecriture," which gave them a wide diffusion.[19] Warburton's pictographic theory remained practically unchallenged for over two hundred years. For example, in the revised edition of *A Study of Writing* (1974), at present one of the best-known modern scholarly publications on writing, I. J. Gelb still stated: "it became clear that the Mesopotamian cuneiform writing has developed from a pictographic stage."[20]

Although the existence of cuneiform had been noticed by Western travelers as early as the fifteenth century, ancient Near Eastern scripts did not play a role in the elaboration of the pictographic theory because they were still little known in 1738. In the nineteenth century, when archaeological expeditions reaped the first great harvests of cuneiform texts and brought them back to Europe, the cuneiform script was regarded as conforming to Warburton's paradigm. In 1913, George A. Barton was of the opinion that "the investigator must proceed upon the hypothesis that Babylonian writing, like other primitive writing, originated in pictographs." The pictographic theory scheme was modified, however, to include a three-step progression from ideographic to phonetic writing. "Indeed," wrote Barton, "wherever the beginnings of writing could be traced, it took the form of picture writing, so that it seems safe to regard it as a working hypothesis, if not as a law, that all early systems of writing began in a series of pictographic ideographs, that syllabic values were developed from these and in some cases alphabetic values."[21]

In fact, the idea that the cuneiform script started with picture writing was by no means a perfect fit. In 1928, a year before the discovery of the Uruk tablets, William A. Mason noted, "We must admit, that even in the earliest and most archaic inscriptions discovered, it is not always easy to recognize the original objects." The pictographic theory, however, was never questioned. Instead, the Babylonian scribes were blamed for the discrepancy between preconceived ideas and facts: "Owing to the limitations of primitive culture, the inexperience of the scribes and the lack of artistic ability, each scribe drew the characters in his own crude, faulty way, often incorrectly; so that it is quite impossible always definitely to distinguish the character and identify it with the object intended."[22]

The season of 1929–1930 at Uruk brought considerable new information about the beginning of writing. Hundreds of archaic tablets were unearthed that pushed writing back to the fourth millennium B.C. Signs traced or impressed with a stylus in a technique different from the cuneiform script had been termed *pictographic*. These archaic tablets, however, contradicted the pictographic theory. Adam Falkenstein, the German scholar who studied the texts, noted that when writing began in Mesopotamia, truly pictorial signs were rare exceptions. Those that were truly pictorial, like the signs for "plow," "chariot," "sledge," or "wild boar," were not only few but of uncommon use, represented by a single occurrence on one tablet alone.[23] The common signs were abstract: the sign for "metal" was a crescent with five lines; the "pictograph" for "sheep" was a circle with a cross. The Uruk tablets seriously strained the pictograph theory by showing that when writing began in Mesopotamia pictographic signs were rarely used.

Edward Chiera and others tried to reconcile Falkenstein's observations with the pictographic theory. They argued that the Uruk texts represented an already evolved script and that a previous stage, consisting of true pictographs, probably had been written on a perishable material, such as wood, bark, papyrus, or parchment which had disintegrated in time and could never be recovered.[24]

The next excavation campaign at Uruk, in 1930–1931, produced impressed tablets which continued to challenge the pictographic theory. These texts, like others found previously at Susa and later at Khafaje, Godin Tepe, Mari, Tell Brak, Habuba Kabira, and Jebel Aruda, were more ancient than the "pictographic" Uruk tablets studied by Falkenstein. They were, however, not made of wood, bark, papyrus, or parchment, as Chiera had hypothesized. This earliest form of writing consisted of wedges, circles, ovals, and triangles impressed on clay tablets and was anything but pictographic. The gulf between the evidence and the neat charts of pictographs illustrated in books became even wider.

By the second half of the twentieth century, enough data had accumulated to present a serious challenge to the pictographic theory. From Champollion in 1822 to Ventris in 1953, each great decipherment eroded the premise upon which the pictographic theory was built and determined that the early scripts all had phonetic features. Anthropologists like André Leroi-Gourhan entered the debate, warning against preconceptions about primitive picture writings. In his volume *Le Geste et la parole*, he argued that "the linguists who have studied the origin of writing have often conferred to pictographic systems a value which derives from literacy." Leroi-Gourhan noted that the only true pictographic scripts were recent phenomena; that most had emerged in groups which did not have writing prior to contacts with travelers or colonists from literate countries. He concluded: "therefore it seems impossible to use Eskimo or Indian pictography in order to understand the ideography of preliterate societies."[25]

Scholars began to question the idea that writing emerged as the rational decision of a group of enlightened individuals, such as that put forward by V. Gordon Childe in *What Happened in History*: "the priests . . . have agreed upon a conventional method of recording receipts and expenditures in written signs that shall be intelligible to all their colleagues and successors; they have invented *writing*."[26] For, like other human inventions, writing did not come *ex nihilo* and, in Chiera's words, "there never was a first man who could sit down and say, 'Now I am going to write.' That supreme achievement of mankind, the one which makes possible the very existence of civilization by transferring to later generations the acquisitions of the earlier ones, was the result of a slow and natural development."[27]

Above all, the pictographic theory was not consistent with modern archaeological research. In recent years, Near Eastern excavations have focused on the beginning of agriculture and cities and have tried to determine how these events affected society. Viewed in the perspective of the urban phenomenon, the first "pictographic" tablets of Uruk (and for that matter the earlier impressed tablets) are out of step with other socioeconomic developments. These first documents occur in level IVa of Uruk, lagging far behind the rise of cities and the emergence of the temple institution, which was already well under way some two hundred years earlier (in levels X–IV). If writing emerged so late, it could not have played a role in state formation. How, then, did the Mesopotamian city-states function without record keeping?

Although popular books have continued to present the traditional pictographic theory,[28] as early as the 1950s scholars had begun to anticipate the discovery of an antecedent of the Mesopotamian script. Some, like V. Gordon Childe, searched for it in seals while others looked into potter's marks, but to no avail.[29] Most, like Seton Lloyd, foresaw an even earlier script: "The degree of competence . . . [attained by script of the Uruk IV tablets] . . . suggests that earlier stages in its development may eventually be recognized elsewhere, perhaps in levels corresponding to Uruk V and VI."[30] David Diringer simply referred to "another more primitive writing" or "an at present unknown, early script, which may have been the common ancestor of [the Indus Valley Script and] also of the cuneiform and early Elamite writings."[31] I propose that the antecedent of writing was not an earlier script, but a counting device. What had been missed—or dismissed—were the humble tokens that had been used for centuries and that were, I argue, the immediate precursor to writing.

The pictographic theory will remain a landmark in the history of ideas because it was the first evolutionary explanation of writing, departing from the former belief that a full-fledged script had been communicated to humans by divine revelation. The theory was based, however, on Egyptian, Chinese, and New World models that were irrelevant. Over the course of the twentieth century, archaeology has generated new evidence that contradicted the paradigm. At the same time, excavations steadily produced small tokens that, as I will show, *were* the antecedent of writing.

TOKENS

The immediate precursor of cuneiform writing was a system of tokens. These small clay objects of many shapes — cones, spheres, disks, cylinders, etc. — served as counters in the prehistoric Near East and can be traced to the Neolithic period, starting about 8000 B.C. They evolved to meet the needs of the economy, at first keeping track of the products of farming, then expanding in the urban age to keep track of goods manufactured in workshops. The development of tokens was tied to the rise of social structures, emerging with rank leadership and coming to a climax with state formation.

Also, corresponding to the increase in bureaucracy, methods of storing tokens in archives were devised. One of these storage methods employed clay envelopes, simple hollow clay balls in which the tokens were placed and sealed. A drawback of the envelopes was that they hid the enclosed tokens. Accountants eventually resolved the problem by imprinting the shapes of the tokens on the surface of the envelopes prior to enclosing them. The number of units of goods was still expressed by a corresponding number of markings. An envelope containing seven ovoids, for example, bore seven oval markings.

The substitution of signs for tokens was a first step toward writing. Fourth-millennium accountants soon realized that the tokens within the envelopes were made unnecessary by the presence of markings on the outer surface. As a result, tablets — solid clay balls bearing markings — replaced the hollow envelopes filled with tokens. These markings became a system of their own which developed to include not only impressed markings but more legible signs traced with a pointed stylus. Both of these types of symbols, which derived from tokens, were picture signs or "pictographs." They were not, however, pictographs of the kind anticipated by Warburton. The signs were not pictures of the items they represented but, rather, pictures of the tokens used as counters in the previous accounting system.

What fascinated me most in this study was the realization that the token system reflected an archaic mode of "concrete" counting prior to the invention of abstract numbers. There were no tokens for "1" or "10." Instead, a particular counter was needed to account for each type of goods: jars of oil were counted with ovoids, small measures of grain with cones, large measures of grain with spheres. Tokens were used in one-to-one correspondence: one jar of oil was shown by one ovoid, two jars of oil by two ovoids, etc. The consequences of this discovery are significant. Namely, writing resulted not only from new bureaucratic demands but from the invention of abstract counting. The most important evidence uncovered is that counting was not, as formerly assumed, subservient to writing; on the contrary, writing emerged from counting.

Studies on Tokens

Tokens came my way by chance. It all started in 1969–1971, when I was awarded a fellowship from the Radcliffe Institute, Cambridge, Massachusetts (now the Bunting Institute) to study the use of clay before pottery in the Near East. This led me to systematically examine Near Eastern archaeological clay collections, dating from 8000 to 6000 B.C., stored in museums of the Near East, North Africa, Europe, and North America. I was looking for bits of Neolithic clay floors, hearth lining, and granaries, for bricks, beads, and figurines, and I found plenty of these. I also came across a category of artifacts that I did not expect: miniature cones, spheres, disks, tetrahedrons, cylinders, and other geometric shapes made of clay. I noted their shape, color, manufacture, and all possible characteristics. I counted them, measured them, drew sketches of them, and entered them into my files under the heading "geometric objects." Later, when it became obvious that not all the artifacts were in geometric form, but some were in the shape of animals, vessels, tools, and other commodities, the word was changed to *token*.

I became increasingly puzzled by the tokens because, wherever I would go, whether in Iraq, Iran, Syria, Turkey, or Israel, they were always present among the early clay assemblages. If they were so widely used, they must have had a useful function. I noted that the tokens were often manufactured with care and that they were the first clay objects to have been hardened by fire. The fact that people went to such trouble for their preparation further suggested that they were of importance. The tokens appeared to be part of a system, for I repeatedly found small and large cones, thin and thick disks, small and large spheres — even fractions of spheres, such as half and three-quarter spheres. But what were the tokens used for?

I asked archaeologists about the tokens and learned that everyone who had excavated early sites had encountered them in their trenches. No one, however, knew what they were. I looked in site reports and noted that tokens were usually omitted or relegated to such headings as "enigmatic objects" or "objects of uncertain purpose." The authors who did risk an interpretation identified the tokens as amulets or game pieces. Carleton Coon is among those who simply wondered. He jovially reported about the five cones he found at Belt Cave, Iran, as follows: "From levels 11 and 12 come five mysterious conical clay objects, looking like nothing in the world but suppositories. What they were used for is anyone's guess."[32]

The data I collected on tokens seemed at first to be of little significance, but ultimately made it possible to recognize the importance of these arti-

of a puzzle that, finally, gave a clue to the entire picture.

Archaeologists

Many archaeologists, starting with Jacques de Morgan at Susa (1905) and Julius Jordan at Uruk (1929), should be recognized for excavating, preserving, and publishing tokens, even though they seemed insignificant at the time. Vivian L. Broman is to be credited for including in her work the study of hundreds of tokens from Jarmo.[33] When Broman completed her thesis in 1958, she too had no alternative but to guess from the shape of the objects what they might have been. Consequently, she attributed a different function to each particular type. She viewed the cones as being perhaps schematic figurines and the spheres as sling stones or marbles. She also earmarked cones, spheres, and hemispheres as possible counters, noting that some Iraqi shepherds today keep track of their flocks with pebbles.[34] At the time, her insight could not be supported by archaeological evidence. Only one year later, however, the use of counters in the ancient Near East was documented.

A. Leo Oppenheim

In 1959, A. Leo Oppenheim of the University of Chicago wrote an article on counters of the second millennium B.C. which proved to be the key to understanding what the tokens were.[35] His paper concerned a peculiar hollow tablet recovered in the late 1920s at the site of Nuzi, in northern Iraq (fig. 2).[36] This egg-shaped tablet belonged, together with a normal tablet bearing an account of the same transaction, in the family archive of a sheep owner named Puhisenni.[37] The cuneiform inscription on the hollow tablet read as follows:

> Counters representing small cattle:
>
> 21 ewes that lamb
> 6 female lambs
> 8 full grown male sheep
> 4 male lambs
> 6 she-goats that kid
> 1 he-goat
> 3 female kids
>
> The seal of Ziqarru, the shepherd.[38]

When opening the hollow tablet, the excavators found it to hold forty-nine counters which, as stipulated in the text, corresponded to the number of animals listed.[39]

That hollow tablet proved to be the Rosetta stone of the token system.

Fig. 2. "Hollow tablet,"
Nuzi, Iraq. Courtesy
Ernest Lacheman.

The counters (Akkadian *abnu*, pl. *abnati*, translated "stone" by Oppenheim), the list of animals, and the explanatory cuneiform text leave no possible doubt that at Nuzi counters were used for accounting. Although no
other example of a cuneiform tablet holding counters has ever been encountered in Nuzi or, for that matter, in Mesopotamia or the Near East, Oppenheim made a case that *abnati* were commonly used in the bureaucracy. He
suggested that each animal of a flock was represented by a stone held in a
container. The tokens were transferred to various receptacles to keep track
of changes of shepherds or pasture, when animals were shorn, and so on.
He based his argument on short cuneiform notes found in archives, referring to *abnati* "deposited," "transferred," and "removed" as follows:

— These sheep are with PN; the (pertinent) stones have not been yet
deposited.
— Three lambs, two young he-goats, the share of PN, they are charged
to his account (but) not deposited among the stones.
— One ewe belonging to PN, its stone has not been removed.
— Altogether 23 sheep of Silwatesup, PN brought . . . their stones have
not been transferred.
— x ewes that have lambed, without (pertaining) stones, belonging
to PN.[40]

Marcel Sigrist has pointed out further texts which probably also allude
to counters in the Third Dynasty of Ur, ca. 2000 B.C. For instance, a tablet
dealing with oxen reads: "The remaining part of the account is held in the
leather pouch" (Sumerian: **Kuš du$_{10}$-gan**).[41]

When Oppenheim wrote his article, no one knew what the counters looked like. Of course, the *abnati* mentioned in the texts were not described and those held in the Nuzi hollow tablet were lost. They were simply referred to as "pebbles" in the site report, with no information as to their shapes or the material of which they were made.[42] The next important piece of the puzzle was provided by Pierre Amiet in Paris.

Pierre Amiet

Pierre Amiet studied seals used in the administration of ancient Near Eastern cultures to validate documents. In particular, he came to study the impressions of such seals on globular clay objects from Susa. These artifacts were hollow and contained small clay objects. Following Oppenheim's lead, Amiet interpreted the small clay objects enclosed in the clay envelopes as "calculi" representing commodities.[43] The proposition was daring, since the Susa envelopes came two thousand years earlier than the Nuzi egg-shaped tablet, with no known example in the interval. It was a leap of great importance for three reasons. First, the counters were revealed: they were miniature clay artifacts modeled in various, mostly geometric, shapes. Second, the Susa envelopes showed that counters held in envelopes were not restricted to the literate period but extended into the time before writing was invented. Third, Amiet foresaw the possibility that the calculi were an antecedent of writing. In his words: "One might ask whether [the scribe] had in mind the little objects that were enclosed in the envelopes, and that very conventionally would symbolize certain goods."[44]

Amiet's contribution was a tremendous step, but it revealed only one time frame of the token system at a particular location: namely, Susa about 3300 B.C. It should be kept in mind that in 1966, prehistoric tokens were not known and the only published parallels to the Susa envelopes were those recently excavated in Uruk.[45] Six years later, in 1972, when Amiet published the Susa envelopes in his *Glyptique susienne*, he still described the markings on envelopes as follows: "a series of round or long notches, similar to the ciphers featured on tablets and corresponding to the number of calculi enclosed inside. The shape of the notches, however, is not as varied as that of the calculi."[46] More recently, Amiet summarized his position: "I was thus wondering whether writing was inspired by certain of these calculi enclosed in the envelopes."[47]

Maurice Lambert, conservator of Western Asiatic antiquities at the Louvre, took Amiet's insight two steps farther. He clearly recognized that the first impressed signs of writing were reproducing the shape of the former calculi: "Writing, here as elsewhere, imitated true things."[48] Consequently, he assigned the values 1, 10, 60, 600, and 3,600 to, respectively, the tetrahedron, sphere, large tetrahedron, punched tetrahedron, and large sphere, a route that turned out to have been, partly, a false one.

The recognition that the tokens constituted an accounting system which existed for five thousand years in prehistory and which was widely used in the entire Near East was to be my own contribution. I was also able to draw parallels between the shapes of the tokens and those of the first incised signs of writing and to establish the continuity between the two recording systems. Finally, much later, I realized the mathematical importance of the tokens as an archaic reckoning device, preceding the invention of abstract counting. I recall vividly when, in 1970, two pieces of the puzzle snapped together for me. In order to prepare a class lecture, I pulled from my files Amiet's 1966 article, which I had not seen since I began collecting tokens. I could not believe my eyes when I saw the small clay cones, spheres, and tetrahedrons illustrating the paper. Until then, I had instinctively dismissed the idea that the Susa artifacts could have anything to do with the tokens which had been found in Neolithic villages. After all, the calculi from Susa were held in envelopes and the Neolithic tokens were loose; moreover, the objects were separated by thousands of years. The next day, however, I was intrigued enough to check several excavation reports of fourth-, fifth-, and sixth-millennium sites and saw the possibility that tokens might have been used, with no discontinuity, between 8000 and 3000 B.C. The rest was hard work. My first publications on tokens and their relation to writing date from 1974 to 1978,[49] those on tokens and concrete counting from 1983 to 1986.[50]

The Evidence PART ONE

What Are Tokens?

CHAPTER ONE

The manufacture of small objects modeled in clay and hardened with fire was a particularly important activity at Tell Aswad, especially in level II, in the first half of the seventh millennium. . . . These were . . . artifacts of geometric shapes, such as balls, disks, and small cups. — HENRI DE CONTENSON[1]

WHEN TOKENS WERE INVENTED, they were great novelties. They were among the first clay objects of the Near East and the first to be fired into ceramic. Their shapes also were revolutionary since, as Cyril Smith has pointed out, they first exploited, systematically, all the basic geometric forms.[2] This first chapter deals with the physical aspect of the tokens, the types and subtypes, the evolution from "plain" to "complex" tokens, the materials of which these artifacts were made, and the technique used for their manufacture.

TYPES AND SUBTYPES

Tokens are small clay objects, modeled into the following sixteen main types: (1) cones, (2) spheres, (3) disks, (4) cylinders, (5) tetrahedrons, (6) ovoids, (7) quadrangles, (8) triangles, (9) biconoids, (10) paraboloids, (11) bent coils, (12) ovals/rhomboids, (13) vessels, (14) tools, (15) animals, and (16) miscellaneous. (See the charts in Part Three below.) The tokens are further classified into subtypes according to intentional variations in size or the addition of markings. Cones, spheres, disks, and tetrahedrons, for example, are consistently represented in two sizes, "small" and "large." Spheres also occur in fractions such as hemispheres and three-quarter spheres. The markings consist of incised lines, notches, punches, pinched appendices, or appliqué pellets.

Because they were handmade, the size of the tokens varies from artifact to artifact and from site to site. The usual dimension ranges from 1 to 3 cm across. The "large" subtypes of cones, spheres, disks, and tetrahedrons measure about 3–5 cm.

EVOLUTION FROM PLAIN TO COMPLEX

During the first four thousand years tokens were "plain" (fig. 3). The forms consisted mainly of geometric shapes, such as cones, spheres, flat and len-

Fig. 3. Plain tokens,
Seh Gabi, Iran.
Courtesy Louis Levine.

ticular disks, cylinders, tetrahedrons (types 1, 2, 3, 4, 5) and only occasionally ovoids, quadrangles, triangles, biconoids, and hyperboloids (types 6, 7, 8, 9, 16). The naturalistic shapes, such as vessels and animals, were also few (types 13, 15). The animal heads consisted of a cone pinched at the top into a beak or a muzzle, sometimes with details such as eyes, ears, or a mustache (type 15: 1−2).[3]

Although some of the earliest assemblages of the eighth millennium B.C. produced a few tokens with an occasional incised line or a punctation, markings remained rare. Plain tokens usually have a smooth face.

After four millennia, the system reached a second stage about 3500 B.C. when new types and subtypes multiplied (fig. 4). These "complex tokens" included new geometric types: paraboloids, bent coils, and ovals/rhomboids (types 10, 11, and 12); ovoids, quadrangles, triangles, and biconoids became more widely used and acquired multiple subtypes (types 6, 7, 8, 9). New naturalistic forms appeared in the shape of miniature tools (type 14), furniture (type 14: 10), fruit, and humans (type 16: 8, 1−3). Lastly, vessels and animals became less schematic (types 13 and 15: 3−13).

The profusion of markings is another distinctive feature of the complex counters. They occur on all types of tokens. Linear markings such as sets of parallel lines and short strokes are most frequently used, but perpendicular lines, stars, checkers, and crisscrossing also occur (some of which are shown in fig. 5). There is also a great variety of punctations (fig. 6). Some consist of deep circular markings, others are small circles or fine pitting done with a needle. The other types of markings—notches, nail incisions, painting, pinching, and appliqué pellets and coils—are rarely used. The tokens provided with appliqué pellets or with pinched appendices may be, in fact, naturalistic representations. For example, the cubes topped by a pellet depict a box secured by sealings. In other words, the tokens are the facsimile of shipments, illustrating the position of strings and sealings (type 7: 25, 26, and 30).

There are, among complex tokens, intriguing series of identical shapes that bear different numbers of lines arranged in similar patterns (chart 1). For example, there are disks displaying sets of 1, 3, 4, 5, 6, 8, or 10 lines (type 3: 19−25). The largest series of disks shows combinations of lines and strokes in various numbers (type 3: 36−48). Triangles and paraboloids occur almost exclusively in series featuring numbers of strokes (type 8: 5−

angles bearing a set of five lines seem to be have been particularly popular
(type 8: 17).

There can be no doubt that plain and complex tokens represent two
steps in the evolution of the same reckoning device. The complex specimens were developed from plain tokens, adopting their size, material, and
method of manufacture. They continued the same basic shapes: namely,
cones, spheres, disks, cylinders, tetrahedrons, ovoids, quadrangles, triangles, vessels, and animal heads. The complex tokens only increased the
repertory of shapes and markings. When the token system started
dwindling, it reverted to a few plain shapes.

The fact that plain and complex tokens were part of the same reckoning
system, used by the same people for the same function, is obvious for several reasons. First, both categories of tokens were found together in the
same sites and hoards and were enclosed in the same envelopes. Second,
they started being perforated at the same time, showing that they were
strung together. Third and finally, plain and complex tokens alike are the
prototypes of pictographs representing basic commodities in the Sumerian
script.

MATERIALS

The material most commonly used for the manufacture of tokens was clay.
In the fourth millennium B.C. tokens were made usually of a very fine paste,
suggesting that the clay was refined. The clay appears to have been worked
while very wet, because traces of fingerprints are frequently visible on the
surface.

There are few examples of plain tokens, and even fewer complex tokens,
made of stone, bitumen, or plaster. Stone tokens are often colorful. They
are made of pink, green, or black marble, white alabaster, grey slate, brown
sandstone, or reddish ocher.

MANUFACTURE

The manufacture of the plain clay tokens was simple. They were shaped by
rolling a small lump of clay between the palms of the hands or pinching it
between the fingertips. All the token forms are very easy to achieve; they
are in fact the shapes which emerge spontaneously when doodling with
clay. Only the tokens of naturalistic shapes representing miniature vessels,
tools, and animals required additional skill for their execution. Markings
were performed either with the fingernail or, more commonly, by tracing
strokes and lines with a pointed instrument.

There are great differences in the care given to the manufacture of tokens
from site to site and even among specimens from the same assemblage.
Most clay tokens are modeled into a well-defined shape with precise and

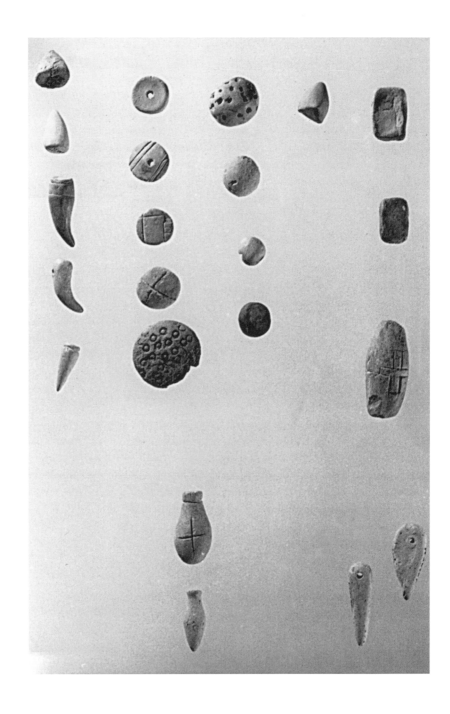

Fig. 4. Token assemblage illustrating major types of tokens, Uruk, Iraq. Courtesy Deutsches Archaeologisches Institut, Abteilung Baghdad.

crisp edges, but some are sloppily done, exhibiting an uneven contour. The stone tokens, which required far greater skill to manufacture and a time-consuming polishing process, usually show excellent craftsmanship.

Tokens of the Neolithic period were not thoroughly baked and often reveal a black core. Scanning electron microscopy and differential thermal analysis confirmed that the firing temperature of the prehistoric tokens varied between 500° and 800° C. The fourth-millennium B.C. counters, on the other hand, are usually buff-pink throughout their thickness, showing a perfect control of the firing process.

THE TOKEN COLLECTION UNDER STUDY

This study is based on 8,162 tokens consisting of 3,354 spheres, 1,457 cones, 1,095 disks, 806 cylinders, 278 quadrangles, 233 triangles, 220 tetrahedrons, 204 ovoids, 129 animals, 85 paraboloids, 81 vessels, 60 bent coils, 51 biconoids, 45 ovals, 33 miscellaneous, and 31 tools. The assemblage, which is fully published in *Before Writing, Volume II: A Catalog of Near Eastern Tokens*, has been compiled by studying the collections in the museums where they were stored or from site reports and, ideally, by combining the two sources.

The catalog suggests two observations. First, the number of tokens differs greatly from site to site. Compare, for example, the largest assemblages—Jarmo 2,022, Uruk 812, Susa 783, Ganj Dareh Tepe 575, Tepe Gawra 485, Tell Ramad 380, and Tell Aswad 320—with some of the smallest collections—Matarrah 1, Tell Songor 1, Ubaid 1, and Tell Hassuna 3. Second, small token assemblages are more frequent than large ones, with as many as thirty collections having fewer than ten tokens.

The number of counters per site does not seem to reflect particular

Fig. 5. Complex tokens, Susa, Iran. Courtesy Musée du Louvre, Département des Antiquités Orientales.

Fig. 6. Tokens with punctated markings, Susa, Iran. Courtesy Musée du Louvre, Département des Antiquités Orientales.

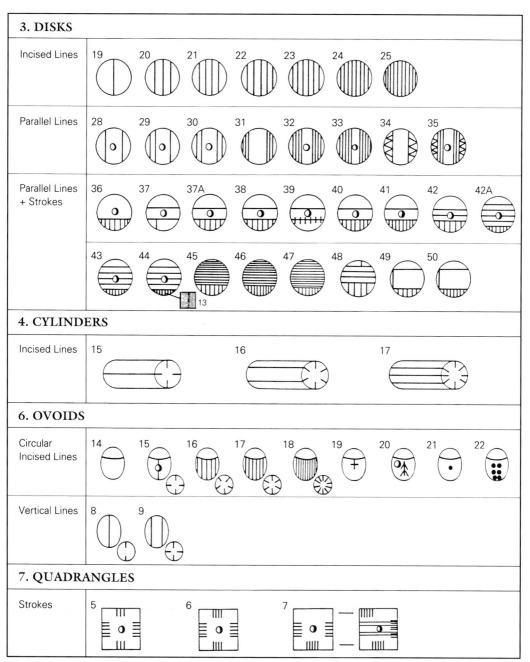

Chart 1. Token series.
Courtesy Deutsches
Archaeologisches
Institut, Abteilung
Baghdad.

Horizontal Lines	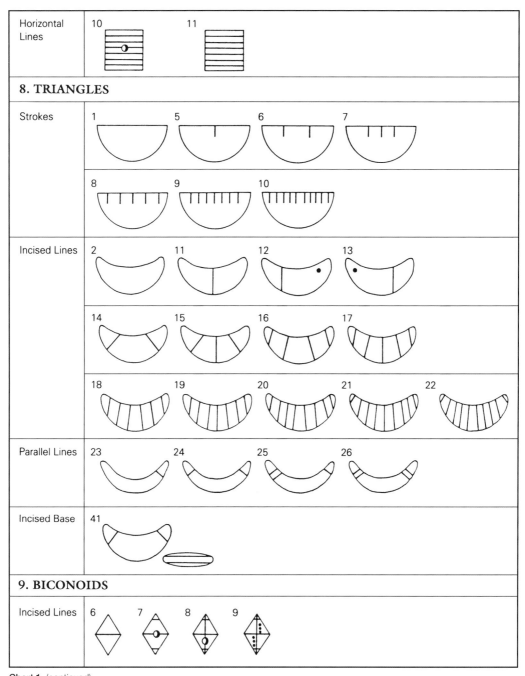

8. TRIANGLES

Strokes	

Incised Lines	

Parallel Lines	

Incised Base	

9. BICONOIDS

Incised Lines	

Chart 1. (continued)

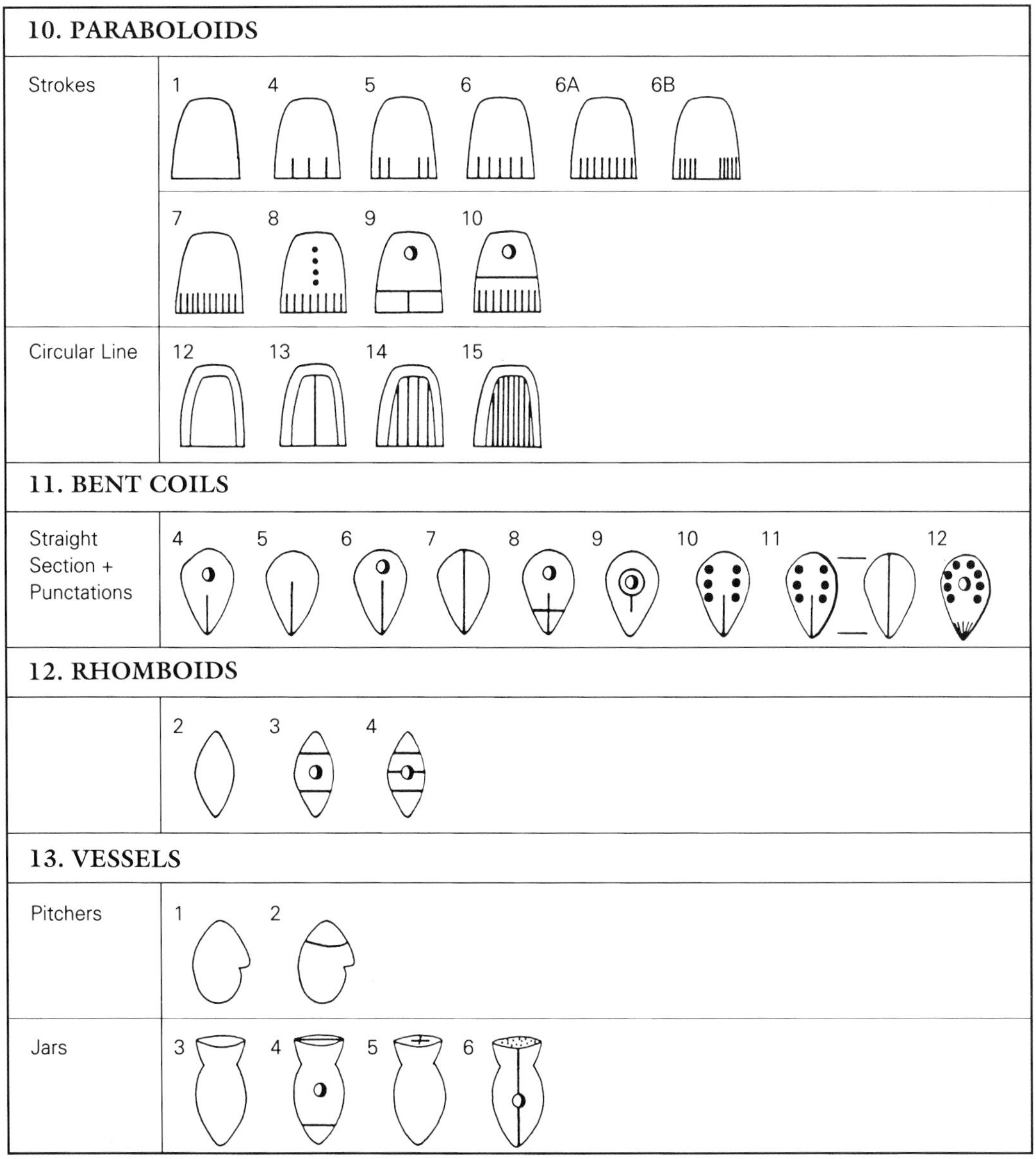

10. PARABOLOIDS

| Strokes | 1 4 5 6 6A 6B |
| 7 8 9 10 |
| Circular Line | 12 13 14 15 |

11. BENT COILS

| Straight Section + Punctations | 4 5 6 7 8 9 10 11 12 |

12. RHOMBOIDS

2 3 4

13. VESSELS

| Pitchers | 1 2 |
| Jars | 3 4 5 6 |

Chart 1. (continued)

socioeconomic factors but, rather, the technical difficulties in excavating the material and in compiling the catalog. There is no indication, for example, that life at Jarmo, which produced some two thousand tokens, was much different from that of other Neolithic sites such as Hassuna, which yielded only three. The large discrepancy between the number of tokens at each site has to do with the type of expedition. Excavations depend greatly upon luck: one trench may produce numerous artifacts, whereas the next is sterile. Consequently, short-term salvage projects limited to small excavated surfaces are more vulnerable to chance than is full-scale horizontal exposure in extensive fieldwork, as at Jarmo. This probably explains why Tell Abada, for example, produced an assemblage of fifty tokens,[4] whereas the neighboring Tell Oueili yielded fewer than five tokens. Methods of excavation are also responsible for the uneven numbers. Tokens pose a challenge to the best excavators because of their size and color. Being small and blending in with the fill, they are particularly difficult to spot. Expeditions such as Jarmo and Ganj Dareh, where the dirt was systematically sifted, had a better chance of salvaging tokens from the excavation dumps than those where this did not occur. At all sites, the plain cylinders—which are not much bigger than a grain of wheat—are probably among those which were most missed. It is very possible that spheres were indeed the most popular token shape; on the other hand, they were often taken for marbles and therefore had the best chance to be entered in site reports under the rubric "games."

In fact, the lack of documentation was the major problem in compiling the token catalog. Often, the tokens are not yet published and thus the collections available represent only a portion of the actual assemblages. This is the case, for instance, for Chogha Mish and Ganj Dareh Tepe. In early excavations, moreover, tokens were glossed over in the site reports. In some cases, the lack of publication could be compensated for by studying the material stored in museums, but more often this could not be done. For example, the following statement in the Hassuna report—"pellets . . . were found in considerable quantities in every level of the main sounding at Hassuna"[5]—suggests that, in fact, many tokens were collected at the site. However, there is no trace of any such artifact at the Iraq Museum, where the Hassuna material is stored, except for one clay cone and two stone spheres. The remainder of the "considerable quantities" of pellets can no longer be accurately documented. The three tokens reported for Hassuna in the catalog are not a representative sample of the original collection.

Hassuna is not the only example where the number of tokens excavated does not correspond to the collections at hand. In fact, this state of affairs is prevalent. Jemdet Nasr, for instance, is another site where, according to the report, cones were found "in great number"; yet only seven specimens are documented.[6] According to M. E. L. Mallowan, cones "were common" at Arpachiyah, but only twenty-four can be traced in the reserves of the British Museum and the Iraq Museum in Baghdad.[7] The reports also often communicate incorrect perceptions. For example, because the stone tokens had more aesthetic appeal than their more modest clay counterparts, they were often given more attention in the publications, sometimes suggesting that stone specimens were more numerous than the clay ones when the reverse was true. At Hassuna, for instance, the only specimens illustrated in the report are two stone spheres.[8] The same thing happens at the site of Amuq and especially at Tepe Gawra, where the stone tokens were published but three hundred clay specimens were dismissed.[9] The Ubaid report includes information on a single token, a paraboloid, described as "the tongue of an animal sculpture."[10] In this case, it is likely that the paraboloid was deemed important enough to be published because its form seemed unusual and interesting, while the more inconspicuous types were ignored. As a result, Ubaid appears, probably erroneously, as a unique assemblage yielding a complex token but no plain ones.

The large number of tokens collected at Jarmo can be explained in several ways. First, Jarmo was a long-term, extensive excavation where the dirt was systematically sifted. Perhaps more important, a member of the team, Vivian L. Broman, was studying clay artifacts. It is likely that her interest generated among the workers the necessary vigilance for finding the objects and keeping them. Furthermore, Broman wrote up her results in her thesis, making the material available.[11] Her study remains unique to this day in presenting a detailed report of a token assemblage. It is obvious that, without Broman's work, we today would know as much—or, rather, as little—about the Jarmo tokens as we do about other Neolithic token assemblages, such as that of Hassuna. The two thousand tokens excavated at Jarmo give us a tantalizing idea of the number of tokens that could be expected at each site. Jarmo was no more and no less than an average farming community in the seventh and sixth millennia B.C. Its token collection should be considered, therefore, as an average Neolithic assemblage. By contrast, the 3 tokens from Hassuna and even the 812 tokens of Uruk, 783 from Susa, and 485 from Tepe Gawra are only a pale reflection of the collections that might have been recovered.

The token assemblages now available give at best precarious and at worst unreliable information on the number of tokens at each site and on the frequency of token types. On the other hand, the same data plotted on a map of the Near East create an awesome picture of the vast geographic expanse where the system of reckoning was used (map 1).

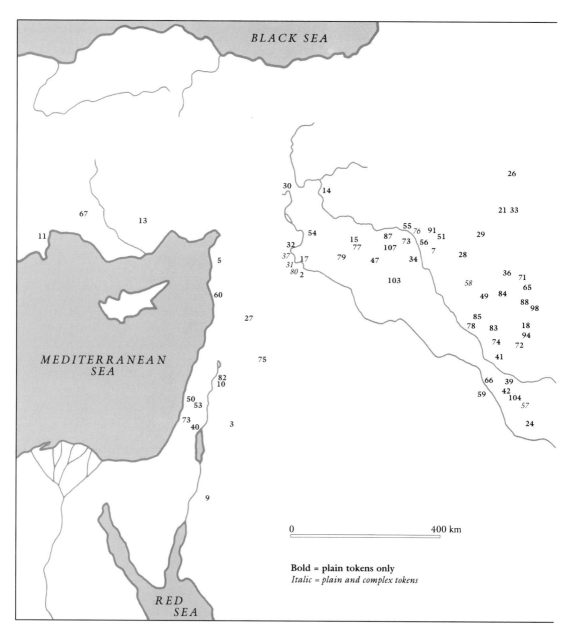

BLACK SEA

MEDITERRANEAN
SEA

RED
SEA

0   400 km

Bold = plain tokens only
Italic = *plain and complex tokens*

1	Abdul Hosein	10	Beisamoun	19	Chogha Bonut	28	Gird Ali Agha	*37*	*Jebel Aruda*	*46*	*Larsa*
2	Abu Hureira	11	Beldibi	*20*	*Chogha Mish*	29	Gird Banahilk	38	Jeitun	47	Maghzaliyah
3	Ain Ghazal	12	Belt Cave	21	Dalma Tepe	30	Gritille	39	Jemdet Nasr	48	Malyan
4	Ali Kosh	13	Can Hasan	22	Deh Luran	*31*	*Habuba Kabira*	40	Jericho	49	Matarrah
5	Amuq	14	Çayönü Tepesi	23	Eridu	32	Hadidi	41	Khafaje	50	Megiddo
6	Anau	15	Chagar Bazar	24	Fara	33	Hajji Firuz	42	Kish	51	M'lefaat
7	Arpachiyah	16	Chagha Sefid	25	Ganj Dareh	34	Hassuna	43	KS 34	*52*	*Moussian*
8	Bampur	17	Cheikh Hassan	26	Geoy Tepe	35	Jaffarabad	*44*	*KS 54*	53	Munhata
9	Beidha	18	Choga Mami	27	Ghoraife	36	Jarmo	45	KS 76	54	Mureybet

Map 1. Distribution of tokens.

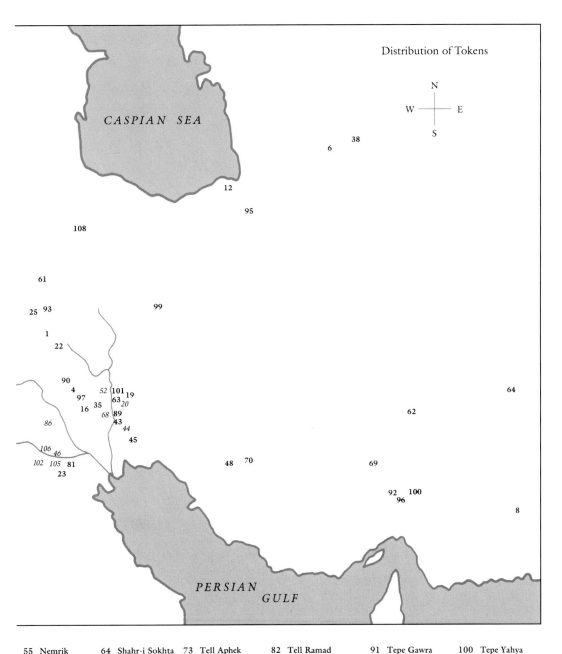

Distribution of Tokens

CASPIAN SEA

PERSIAN GULF

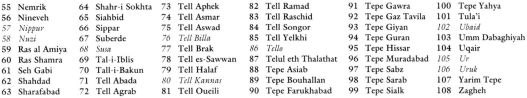

55	Nemrik	64	Shahr-i Sokhta	73	Tell Aphek	82	Tell Ramad	91	Tepe Gawra	100	Tepe Yahya
56	Nineveh	65	Siahbid	74	Tell Asmar	83	Tell Raschid	92	Tepe Gaz Tavila	101	Tula'i
57	*Nippur*	66	Sippar	75	Tell Aswad	84	Tell Songor	93	Tepe Giyan	*102*	*Ubaid*
58	*Nuzi*	67	Suberde	*76*	*Tell Billa*	85	Tell Yelkhi	94	Tepe Guran	103	Umm Dabaghiyah
59	Ras al Amiya	*68*	*Susa*	77	Tell Brak	*86*	*Tello*	95	Tepe Hissar	104	Uqair
60	Ras Shamra	69	Tal-i-Iblis	78	Tell es-Sawwan	87	Telul eth Thalathat	96	Tepe Muradabad	*105*	*Ur*
61	Seh Gabi	70	Tall-i-Bakun	79	Tell Halaf	88	Tepe Asiab	97	Tepe Sabz	*106*	*Uruk*
62	Shahdad	71	Tell Abada	*80*	*Tell Kannas*	89	Tepe Bouhallan	98	Tepe Sarab	107	Yarim Tepe
63	Sharafabad	72	Tell Agrab	81	Tell Oueili	90	Tepe Farukhabad	99	Tepe Sialk	108	Zagheh

Map 1. (continued)

Where Tokens Were Handled and Who Used Them

There is one fact which can be established: the only phenomena which, always and in all parts of the world, seems to be linked with the appearance of writing . . . is the establishment of hierarchical societies, consisting of masters and slaves, and where one part of the population is made to work for the other part.

— CLAUDE LÉVI-STRAUSS [1]

THIS CHAPTER IS DEVOTED to recounting the contexts in which tokens have been recovered. I describe the types of settlements and structures where tokens were found and the artifacts with which they were associated. Finally, I focus on the rare tokens discovered in funerary contexts because these may yield important information concerning the status of the individuals with whom they were buried.

TYPES OF SETTLEMENTS

The five sites where tokens first appeared around 8000 B.C. — Tepe Asiab and Ganj Dareh E in Iran[2] and Tell Aswad, Tell Mureybet, and Cheikh Hassan in Syria[3] — were remarkably similar. All were small open-air compounds built with characteristic round huts. Among them, the two Iranian settlements were semipermanent, but Tell Mureybet, Cheikh Hassan, and Tell Aswad were fully sedentary, agricultural communities. During the seventh to fourth millennia B.C., tokens spread to a great diversity of habitats. In Iran, Belt Cave (inhabited during the Neolithic period) and Tula'i, an encampment of nomadic herders, both yield clay counters.[4] The majority of plain tokens, however, come from sedentary villages of rectangular houses, such as Jarmo in Iraq.

On the other hand, complex tokens are associated with the ruins of cities having monumental public architecture. This is the case for Uruk, in Iraq, Susa, in Iran, and Habuba Kabira, in Syria.

DISTRIBUTION WITHIN SETTLEMENTS

In most of the sites where the context of tokens was recorded, the counters were recovered partly within and partly outside buildings. At Tell Aswad, as at other sites, a good many tokens were located in vacant lots, mixed with animal bones and other debris, in what appear to be trash deposits.[5] At Sharafabad in the fourth millennium B.C., tokens were retrieved from an ancient garbage pit, where it could be determined that the counters were most often associated with early summer deposits but were rarer in layers corresponding to winter trash. Henry T. Wright noted that tokens were apparently discarded after the harvest, the traditional season for feasts.[6]

Both in Uruk and in Susa tokens were found in close proximity to the main temples. In Uruk, counters were spotted all over the tell, but 719 examples (88.5%) were excavated in the sacred precinct of Eanna, 43 (5.3%) came from the Anu Ziggurat, and 50 (6.2%) were from the city's private quarters. It also seems significant that at Susa almost every single trench opened south of the main temple generated tokens, but only a few were recovered in the northern part of the same tell of the Acropolis and in the next tell of the Ville Royale. In both cities, tokens were found in open spaces. At Eanna, tokens were scattered about on the grounds of the Stone Cone Temple[7] and in the Great Courtyard.[8]

The distribution of tokens within settlements suggests two important facts. First, in cities, tokens are more frequent in official rather than secular quarters. Second, the discovery of tokens among refuse in vacant lots suggests that the counters were discarded as soon as their function had been fulfilled. In other words, they were used primarily for record keeping rather than for reckoning. In this regard, the tokens are similar to the archaic tablets of Uruk, also consistently found in dumps, and remind us of the custom that continued in historic times of routinely discarding economic tablets.[9]

STRUCTURES

The structures which yielded tokens fall into two categories: domestic and public. At Ali Kosh, a few tokens were retrieved from a domestic setting, where they were associated with flint tools and with ground stone mortars and pestles.[10] In this case, the tokens give the impression of having been discarded when the house was no longer in use, rather than being *in situ*. The same is true at Seh Gabi, where some tokens were scattered among ordinary houses — here next to a jar,[11] there in a hearth.[12] At Tell es-Sawwan,[13] Hajji Firuz,[14] and Gaz Tavila[15] the tokens were concentrated in storage areas. This was also the case at Ganj Dareh Tepe, where a large quantity of tokens lay among cubicles situated below the houses.[16]

The most interesting finding at Hajji Firuz consisted of a cluster of six cones located in a structure showing no trace of domestic activities, such as cooking or flint chipping.[17] The building also differed from the remaining houses in other ways. First, it was smaller, consisting of a single room instead of the normal two-room unit. Second, unusual features, such as a low platform and two posts had been erected inside.[18] The structure which yielded most tokens at Hajji Firuz apparently served a special, albeit enigmatic, function. At Tell Abada, the majority of the tokens, a total of forty artifacts, sometimes kept in vessels, were recovered in Building A, the largest building excavated in the settlement. The size of the building

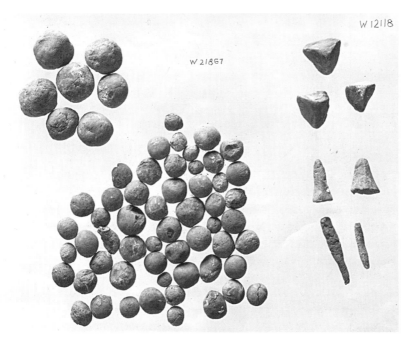
W 21867

W 12118

Fig. 7. Cache of tokens
found in a hearth, Uruk
(Oa XV 4/5), Iraq.
Courtesy Deutsches
Archaeologisches
Institut, Abteilung
Baghdad.

and the presence of infant burials suggested to the excavators "a religious significance."[19]

At Uruk, tokens were related to some of the most spectacular buildings of level V, such as the Stone Cone Temple and the Limestone Temple, but the trenches laid in the city yielded exceedingly few counters. A cache of seventy-five tokens was recovered *in situ* in the impressive complex of Buildings F, G, and H of Eanna (fig. 7). These structures, erected at right angles around a courtyard, were typical of the monumental architecture at Eanna. They were built according to the usual plan, which consisted of a large central hall flanked by smaller rooms, and their facades were decorated with niches. The sixty-one spheres, seven large spheres, three tetrahedrons, two cones, and two cylinders lay on the floor of a room extending to the north of Building H, in a large circular hearth with a long appendix of the *Pfannenstiel* type.[20] It is puzzling that tokens were located in fireplaces on two occasions, at Seh Gabi and Uruk. It might be hypothesized that they were intentionally placed in the hearth in order to be baked. On the other hand, it is also possible and perhaps more likely that they were brushed into the ashes with other trash in order to be discarded.

At Susa, tokens also belonged to the temple precinct, where they were clustered in a zone devoted to workshops and warehouses. For example, Mecquenem indicates that envelopes holding tokens were excavated in a storage area.[21] The structures, made of clay and involving decorations made with large cones, were divided into small compartments. One of these houses was still filled with long-spouted jars that held a black, powdery substance.

Seven of the largest and most imposing houses of Habuba Kabira yielded tokens. These buildings stood out because of their typical Sumerian floor plan and central courtyards. Most of these buildings produced other bureaucratic materials such as seals and sealings, oblong bullae, envelopes, and impressed tablets. Otherwise, flint tools, pottery, and spindle whorls seem to indicate domestic concerns. It seems particularly significant that the southern city gate, which led to the temple, produced not only fifteen tokens but a cylinder seal and numerous oblong bullae.

In sum, tokens were often located in storage facilities and warehouses. More important, there is evidence that as early as the sixth millennium B.C. tokens also occur in nondomestic architecture. These public buildings can take the form, over time, of a "temple" as at Uruk or of a city gate as at Habuba Kabira.

TOKEN CLUSTERS

Tokens are frequently found in groups varying from two to about one hundred. At Gaz Tavila, thirty-five cones and one sphere were nestled together in the corner of a storeroom.[22] Ganj Dareh Tepe also produced many small hoards of two to thirty-seven tokens of mixed types, tightly packed together in storage cubicles. Tell Abada yielded eleven clusters of four to sixteen tokens.[23] Finally, Uruk produced the cache of seventy-five tokens composed of spheres, large spheres, cones, tetrahedrons, and cylinders described above. Moreover, there can be little doubt that some of the 155 tokens from level VI of Eanna were also clustered together.

The groups of tokens recovered in the buildings of Habuba Kabira were remarkably small. The house which yielded the largest number produced twenty-one, divided into five rooms in clusters of at most nine tokens. Furthermore, except for House 2, which held only incised ovoids, the assemblages were always composed of several types of counters. In sum, the evidence indicates that the accounts kept with tokens dealt generally with rather small quantities of different kinds of commodities.

CONTAINERS HOLDING TOKENS

At Tell Abada, some tokens were held in pottery bowls or jars and others were found on the floor.[24] In most other sites, the tokens were located on the floor of the buildings or storage cubicles. Because they were clustered tightly together it is likely that they had been held in a container which disintegrated in time, leaving no trace. Baskets, wooden boxes, leather or textile pouches are among the possible types of receptacles which might have been used. In texts from the Third Dynasty of Ur, ca. 2000 B.C., there is perhaps a reference to leather bags being used to hold tokens. Marcel

Sigrist has noted a tablet referring to "1492 fat oxen in the leather bag" which, according to Sigrist, can be understood as "counters representing 1492 oxen kept in archive in a leather bag."[25]

ASSOCIATED ASSEMBLAGES

In the eighth millennium B.C. the first tokens coincide with food production. The fact that counting and accounting were related to agriculture is particularly well illustrated at Mureybet. Here, the first occurrence of tokens (in level III) corresponded with a quantum jump in the quantity of cereal pollen. This implies the cultivation of grain in fields, whereas wild grains were still being gathered in the previous levels (II and I), when tokens were not yet in use. Also, Mureybet III initiated large rectangular silos to store cereals.[26] Finally, the settlement expanded rapidly, reflecting a population increase.[27] Subsistence also relied upon grain consumption at Ganj Dareh Tepe, Tepe Asiab, Tell Aswad, and Cheikh Hassan. On the other hand, none of these five sites, except perhaps Tepe Asiab,[28] provided any osteological evidence for domestication of animals. From the seventh to the early fourth millennium B.C., tokens continued to be typical of agricultural communities. Tokens were apparently not related to trade in general or to the obsidian trade in particular. There was no obsidian at Ganj Dareh Tepe, which produced many tokens. Mureybet I and II worked the prized volcanic glass before tokens came into existence.

In the fourth millennium B.C. the five sites which produced the largest assemblages of complex tokens — Uruk and Tello in Iraq, Susa and Chogha Mish in Iran, and Habuba Kabira–Tell Kannas in Syria — have strikingly similar assemblages. Although the cities were separated by several hundred miles, they shared the same characteristic monumental architecture, decorated with niches and clay cone mosaics.[29] The assemblages also yielded identical pottery vessels in the same typical shapes and decorations, such as four-lugged jars with painted and incised motifs.[30] Each of the sites held, in particular, a great number of crudely manufactured beveled-rim bowls which may have served as measures for the distribution of food rations.[31] The seals and sealings of the five cities were alike, bearing similar motifs. They featured the bearded figure of the Mesopotamian priest-king, the so-called En, in his typical attire consisting of a long robe in a netlike fabric and a round headdress.[32] Finally, all five sites except Tello yielded not only envelopes holding tokens but impressed tablets as well. The various features which occur with consistency in the assemblages of sites yielding complex tokens — the priest-king, public monumental architecture, measures, seals, and complex tokens — represent the elements of an elaborate bureaucracy. They indicate the presence of a powerful economic institution headed by an En, who acted in public buildings decorated with mosaics and relied upon a control of goods involving seals, beveled-rim bowls, and complex tokens.

It is significant that the architecture decorated with cone mosaics, the beveled-rim bowls, the cylinder seals, and the motif of the En are of Mesopotamian origin but were foreign in Iran and Syria. In fact, they were hallmark features of the precinct of Eanna at Uruk. From this perspective, it may be particularly significant that the large collection of tokens in level VI was associated with the piles of clay cone mosaics marking the first evidence for decorated public buildings at Eanna.[33] Whereas agriculture is the major common denominator between sites yielding plain tokens, the cities that produced complex tokens shared the same bureaucracy, which had special ties with South Mesopotamia.

TOKENS AS FUNERARY OFFERINGS

On rare occasions, counters were associated with funerary deposits. These burials may provide information on the individuals who were utilizing tokens.

The Sites

From the sixth to the fourth millennia B.C., tokens were sometimes laid in burials. Among the five sites which furnished tokens in a funerary context, Tell es-Sawwan, Arpachiyah, and Tepe Gawra are located in northern Mesopotamia;[34] Tepe Guran and Hajji Firuz are in Iran.[35] The custom was practiced, therefore, in a widespread geographic area and cannot be considered a regional development.

The Burials

At each of the five sites, the number of sepultures provided with tokens is very small. Only four out of some one hundred thirty burials excavated in Tell es-Sawwan I yielded counters. There was a single case of tokens laid as grave gifts among, respectively, the fourteen interments of Hajji Firuz, the fifty Ubaid graves of Arpachiyah, the thirty graves of Tepe Gawra XVII, and the five graves of Tepe Gawra XI. Finally, only four out of eighty tombs of Tepe Gawra X held counters. The total number of burials including tokens, then, amounts to no more than a dozen.

The interments provided with counters were of several types. At Hajji Firuz, tokens were mixed with the disarticulated bones of a multiple burial;[36] at Tell es-Sawwan, Arpachiyah, and Tepe Gawra XVII and XI, tokens were part of simple graves consisting of a shallow pit dug in the earth.[37] Finally, in Tepe Gawra X, tokens were laid in elaborate tombs involving a brick or stone enclosure.[38]

The various sepultures furnished with tokens belonged to adult males or children, except in the case of Hajji Firuz, where one of the four individuals of the ossuary may have been a young female.[39] It is striking that nearly all these sepultures yielding tokens show some unusual features. A first group of burials is characterized by being lavishly furnished. Among them, the graves of Tell es-Sawwan had quantities of alabaster vessels and, in two cases, ornaments of either dentalia shell or carnelian.[40] At Tepe Gawra, the child grave in stratum XI was unique in holding gold ornaments.[41] In level X of Tepe Gawra, Tombs 102, 110, and 114 were among the richest sepultures of the site. They included obsidian, serpentine, or electrum vessels, gold ornaments in the form of studs, beads, or rosettes, stone maceheads, and lapis lazuli seals.[42]

A second group of burials was associated with uncommon architectural features. For example, at Hajji Firuz, the human bones deposited with tokens were in the small, unusual building described above.[43] The second example, Tomb 107 at Tepe Gawra, was the sepulture of an adult male who was unique in having a shrine erected upon his remains.[44] In this case, the burial gifts amounted to six spheres — and nothing else (fig. 8). Finally, the most puzzling burial, the grave of Tepe Gawra XVII, belonged to an individual with both legs amputated below the knee.[45] The burial at Arpachiyah

Fig. 8. Details of selected tomb burials (Tombs 102, 107, 110, 114). Reproduced from Arthur J. Tobler, *Excavations at Tepe Gawra,* vol. 2, University Museum Monographs (Philadelphia: University of Pennsylvania Press, 1950), pl. XXVII; courtesy University Museum, University of Pennsylvania.

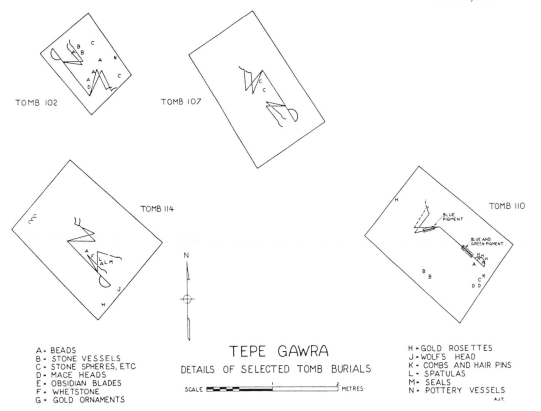

TOMB 102

TOMB 107

TOMB 114

TOMB 110

N

TEPE GAWRA

DETAILS OF SELECTED TOMB BURIALS

SCALE   METRES

A - BEADS
B - STONE VESSELS
C - STONE SPHERES, ETC
D - MACE HEADS
E - OBSIDIAN BLADES
F - WHETSTONE
G - GOLD ORNAMENTS

H - GOLD ROSETTES
J - WOLFS HEAD
K - COMBS AND HAIR PINS
L - SPATULAS
M - SEALS
N - POTTERY VESSELS

A.J.T.

is the only one which yields tokens but has no other particularly striking
features.

The Tokens

Among the many types and subtypes of tokens, four only were recovered
in sepultures: cones, spheres, three-quarter spheres, and miniature vessels.
Among these, spheres were by far most frequently used, occurring in ten of
the fourteen burials with a total number of forty-nine specimens. The forty-
four cones were distributed among only three sepultures, and three-quarter
spheres and vessels were present in a single grave.

As a rule, only one kind of token was usually represented in each burial.
For example, three graves of Tell es-Sawwan contained spheres, but the
fourth grave held a cone;[46] Tombs 107 and 110 of Tepe Gawra held only
spheres, but the grave in level XVII held cones.[47] Tomb 102 of Tepe Gawra,
however, yielded both spheres and cones.[48]

Tokens laid in burials were identical in shape to those found in settlements. The only difference between tokens used as funerary offerings and
those used in daily life is that the former were often made of stone instead
of clay. Nine of the fourteen sepultures were provided with stone tokens,
for a total of sixty-six stone specimens against forty-one made of clay. The
stone examples were usually done with great care and show superb work-
manship. The spheres, for example, are perfectly round. There is one case
at Tepe Gawra, however, when spherical counters — referred to as "pebbles"
in the report — were left rough.[49] In another instance, six chips of red jas-
per were seemingly intended to be made into counters, but were never finished.[50] It is possible that the color of stone selected for the manufacture of
tokens was meaningful: all spheres were white with the exception of two
sets of red spheres (or "pebbles")[51] and a single black specimen.[52] The number of tokens included in each sepulture varied from a minimum of one
sphere at Arpachiyah to a maximum of thirty-four cones in Tepe Gawra
XVII. Sets of six spheres ("pebbles") which reoccur in three out of four
tombs of Tepe Gawra X, suggest that this number may have had a symbolic
significance.

The ritual of depositing in burials tokens of special types, material, color
and, in particular, number is especially significant, since it lasted for three
millennia in several regions of the Near East. Notably, as will be discussed
in Chapter 6 below, this ritual gives a valuable insight into the important
role of the tokens as status symbols. The fact that tokens occur only in rare
occasions in a funerary setting, and only in graves of prestigious individuals, points to their economic significance. It implies that the tokens were
a means of controlling goods in the hands of powerful people.

A FAINT SKETCH of the places and people associated with the use of tokens
begins to emerge. Plain tokens began to be used in open-air compounds
where subsistence was based on cultivating or, at least, hoarding grain;

complex tokens were the invention of the South Mesopotamian temples.
The plain specimens remained a familiar feature in agricultural communities until the end of the system, whereas the complex ones occur only in administrative centers. Starting in the fifth millennium, tokens are consistently found in public buildings and warehouses. When they are in a domestic setting, the counters tend to be clustered in storage areas. The hoards of tokens found *in situ* range usually from twelve to seventy-five artifacts, showing that both in private and public buildings the counters were never kept in large quantities. They may have been stored in leather pouches until the invention of the cylinder seal ushered in the invention of clay envelopes and bullae. Tokens were apparently not reused but were disposed of once the transaction they represented was concluded. There is even some evidence that the counters were discarded after the harvest. Tokens, together with other status symbols, were sometimes included in the burials of prestigious individuals, suggesting that they were used by members of the elite.

Strings of Tokens and Envelopes

When shaking . . . [the clay balls] . . . close to the ear, one can hear the noise of the small objects knocking against one another inside. Specimens, broken in the course of the excavations, showed that they contained small terra-cotta artifacts of various shapes: grains, cones, pyramids, pills 1 cm in diameter. — R. DE MECQUENEM[1]

IN THE EARLY FOURTH MILLENNIUM B.C. two methods were devised to store tokens in archives. The first consisted of tying perforated tokens with a string; the second, enclosing the counters in clay envelopes. Both techniques insured that groups of tokens representing one account could be securely held together and that the transaction could be identified by sealings. Interest in these two devices would be esoteric if it were not for their importance in the invention of writing.

STRINGS OF TOKENS

Perforated Tokens

Some tokens show a perforation throughout their thickness (fig. 9). The geographic and chronological distribution of these perforated artifacts suggests that they were not a general phenomenon but were restricted to complex token assemblages. The geographic distribution of perforated tokens is close to that of complex tokens. There are no perforated specimens in Turkey or Palestine, but some are represented in particular sites in Iraq, Iran, and Syria. Perforated tokens occur occasionally in plain token collections of the early periods, but they proliferate in the fourth millennium B.C. There are, for example, 119 perforated tokens at Uruk, representing 14.7 percent of the assemblage, 189 at Susa (27 percent), and 118 at Habuba Kabira (84 percent).

Solid Bullae

The perforations apparently allowed a string or thong to hold the tokens of a particular transaction together. If this idea is correct, we may expect that both ends of the string were tied together and secured by sealings identifying the account and preventing any tampering. A category of small bullae, bearing sealings, could have served this purpose (figs. 10 and 11). The bullae are made of clay. They are solid, modeled in an oblong or biconoid shape, measure about 7 cm in length and 5 cm in diameter. The bullae are covered with sealings and show, at both ends, the trace of the strings to which they were attached.

Bullae are generally viewed as tags tied onto bales of merchandise.[2] Their interpretation as a device for holding tokens is supported by the fact that the geographic distribution of the bullae also generally coincides with that of complex tokens. At Susa,[3] Chogha Mish,[4] and Habuba Kabira,[5] for example, complex tokens and solid bullae belong to the same horizon and in the same vicinity, although there is no reference in the reports that they were found in direct association.[6] It may be significant that the greatest

Fig. 9. Disks (some perforated), Uruk, Iraq. Courtesy Vorderasiatisches Museum, Staatliche Museen zu Berlin.

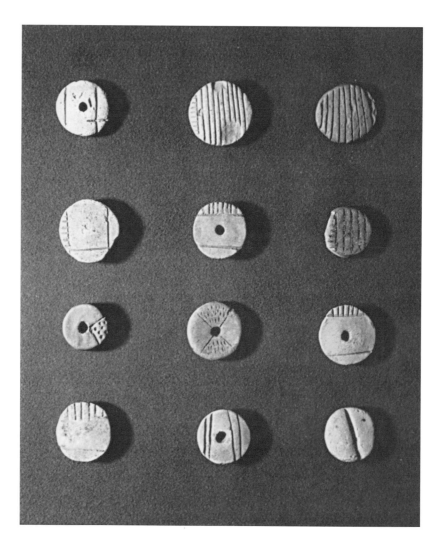

number of bullae comes from Habuba Kabira, the site that produced the most perforated tokens, and that none has yet been recovered at Uruk, where perforated tokens were few. Furthermore, as shown by the imprints at both extremities of the bullae, the strings they held were thin and could fit easily in the token perforations. Finally, their close resemblance to the envelopes described below cannot be coincidental. The two kinds of objects are very similar in appearance: they are made of the same material, share the same size and, sometimes, are modeled in the same oblong shapes. They also bear the same sealings, showing similar motifs, including lines of peaceful animals, lions in heraldic posture, and humans performing tasks. In some instances, in fact, an impression of the same seal appears on both types of artifacts. For example, at Susa, a particular seal featuring a line of

Fig. 10. Two bullae, Susa (Sb 6298 and 9279), Iran. Courtesy Musée du Louvre, Département des Antiquités Orientales.

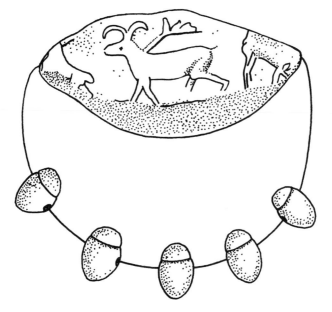

Fig. 11. Proposed reconstruction of a string of tokens held by a solid bulla. Drawing by Ellen Simmons.

peaceful animals and a line of felines was impressed on a solid bulla as well as on two envelopes.[7] The number of seals is also the same on solid bullae and envelopes: both have mostly the impression of a single seal rolled all over their surfaces and, on occasion, two or three. In addition, a few examples of solid bullae at Susa, Habuba Kabira, Tell Brak, and Chagar Bazar feature impressed markings like those borne by some of the envelopes, as will be described later in this chapter.[8] As discussed below, moreover, some of the envelopes may also have involved a system of stringing tokens.

The two kinds of artifacts have two main differences, however. First, the envelopes were hollow and the bullae were solid. Second, the envelopes were preferred for storing plain tokens, whereas complex specimens were mostly strung. To be exact, 83.69 percent of the tokens contained in envelopes were plain and 10.57 percent were complex (5.74 percent remain undetermined). In addition, there are more perforated tokens among complex specimens than there are among plain specimens. It should be emphasized here, however, that there was cross-over between the two methods. Incised ovoids, which are complex tokens, were held in envelopes from Habuba Kabira and Uruk; punched cones and tetrahedrons, triangles, rectangles, paraboloids, and animals were held in envelopes from either Susa or Uruk, or from both. On the other hand, thirteen plain specimens from Uruk were perforated, as were forty-five at Habuba Kabira (including thirty-five cones) and fourteen at Susa.

In sum, the envelopes and bullae are closely related in shape and function, and it is likely that they represent two alternative ways of identifying and protecting tokens to be held in archives. For reasons that we do not know, plain tokens were most often secured by envelopes and complex tokens by solid bullae.

ENVELOPES

The Artifacts

The envelopes consist of spherical or ovoid hollow clay balls measuring about 5–7 cm (fig. 12). Their manufacture was simple. The cavity to hold the tokens was shaped by poking a hole into a ball of clay with the fingers, as is shown by traces of fingertips visible inside. The red color of some of the envelopes suggests that the artifacts were baked. The fact that envelopes were fired was confirmed by electron microscopy and differential thermal analysis performed on a sample from Susa.[9] Like tokens, the envelopes were baked at a low temperature of about 700° C.

Geographic Distribution and Number

Five out of the eleven protoliterate sites which produced envelopes are located in Iran. These sites are Shahdad, Tepe Yahya, Chogha Mish, Susa, and Farukhabad. One is in Iraq (Uruk), one in Saudi Arabia (Dharan), one

Fig. 12. Envelope with six incised ovoids (the full content of the envelope was seven incised ovoids), Uruk (W 20987.7), Iraq. Courtesy Deutsches Archaeologisches Institut, Abteilung Baghdad.

in Israel (Dumah), and three in Syria (Habuba Kabira, Tell Sheikh Hassan, and Tell Qraya). The distribution of the envelopes is thus spread over a large region which stretches from Iran to the Levant and from Iraq to Saudi Arabia (map 2).

The total number of envelopes now known is about 130 specimens and 70 fragments. The majority, or around 100 complete envelopes and 70 fragments, representing 85 percent of the total assemblage, come from Iran. Among the Iranian sites, Susa produced 40 complete, 15 fragmentary envelopes, and 57 fragments.[10] The assemblage of Chogha Mish is still unpublished, except for 8 complete envelopes recovered in the second campaign and a hoard of more than 20 during the third.[11] Finally, Farukhabad, Tepe Yahya, and Shahdad each produced 1 example.[12] Iraq has a total of 25 envelopes, all of which come from Uruk.[13] Syria yielded 2 at Habuba Kabira and 3 at Tell Sheikh Hassan.[14] The number of envelopes excavated at Tell Qraya is undisclosed.[15] The specimen from Israel, which was purchased on the antiquity market, was said to belong to a lot of 2, originating from the site of Dumah, near Hebron.[16] The single envelope from Saudi Arabia is a surface find, collected near the Dharan airport.[17]

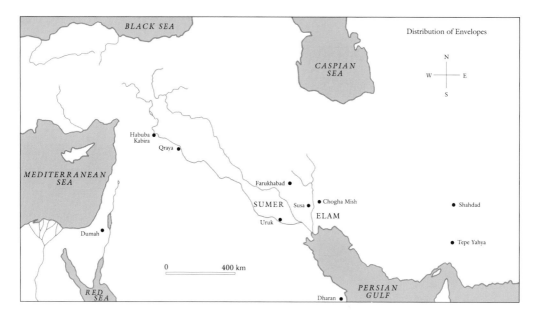

Map 2. Distribution of
envelopes.

Chronology

The envelopes were in use for at least several centuries. They began being
used in the Middle Uruk period, about 3700–3500 B.C., as shown by the
Farukhabad[18] and Chogha Mish examples.[19] They persisted until ca.
2600 B.C. at Tepe Yahya.[20] The custom of marking the artifacts started as
early as Eanna VI–V, about 3500 B.C., as seen at Habuba Kabira.[21] This
date is consistent with the information provided by the excavations at Susa,
where seventeen envelopes originated in level 18[22] and one in level 17,[23] now
equated repectively to Eanna VI and V.[24] Consequently, we know the envelopes of Susa to be contemporaneous with those of Habuba Kabira. It is
interesting to note that some of the envelopes of level 18 were inscribed, but
the example of level 17 was not.[25] The markings, therefore, were not a function of time. The discovery of the Uruk clay cases in the Stone Cone Temple
area also suggests a date as early as Eanna VI–V.

Context

The majority of the envelopes were associated with artifacts typical of
Eanna VI–IV and were connected with the South Mesopotamian temple
bureaucracy. At Uruk, the twenty-five envelopes were found tucked in
a wall in the vicinity of the Stone Cone Temple in the temple precinct
of Inanna. This suggests that the envelopes were part of the Stone Cone
Temple archives and had been discarded, together with tokens, sealings,

and beveled-rim bowls,[26] once the site was abandoned and became a quarry and dumping ground.

The envelopes of Susa, like those of Uruk, came from an area close to an important temple. According to Mecquenem the area where the artifacts were found was occupied by buildings divided into small compartments, presumably temple warehouses or workshops.[27] In the more recent campaigns, seventeen envelopes with other administrative material (including solid oblong bullae, impressed tablets, and beveled-rim bowls) came from a building some 30 m away from the monumental terrace of the temple; it is highly probable that the building fulfilled some temple function.[28]

At Habuba Kabira, the two envelopes were unearthed in the largest and most imposing house of the city. It was one of several structures at the site that were laid out according to a plan familiar in South Mesopotamia but unusual in Syria, with small rooms organized around a central courtyard. The building produced not only the two envelopes and their contents of incised ovoids but various articles used in administration, such as seals and sealings, complex tokens, oblong solid bullae, and four impressed tablets. The function of the building was certainly related in some fashion to a South Mesopotamian administration.

The setting of Tepe Yahya was similar to that of Uruk, Susa, or Habuba Kabira. It too involved an administrative building, which held plain tokens, tablets, beveled-rim bowls, nose-lugged jars, seals, and sealings.[29] In this case, however, the seals and sealings were typically Elamite and the tablets bore accounts written in the Proto-Elamite script. Tepe Yahya shows that envelopes appeared in two settings: related either to the South Mesopotamian temple bureaucracy or the Proto-Elamite bureaucracy.

State of Preservation

The envelopes have been recovered in various states of preservation. Some eighty are still intact, keeping and hiding an unknown number of tokens. Several of the pieces found whole have been subsequently opened by various methods in order to see their contents (table 1). Among them, four envelopes from Susa were punctured with a knife,[30] whereas the specimen from Tepe Yahya was carefully cut open at one extremity. As a result, the number of envelopes whose contents are known with absolute certainty amounts to no more than five, or a mere 3 percent of the known assemblage.

Other envelopes were broken in antiquity but were still associated with their full or partial contents of tokens (table 2). This is the case for nineteen examples from Susa, an unknown number from Chogha Mish, five in Uruk, and two in Habuba Kabira.[31] At Farukhabad, the broken envelope was separated from its contents, but the mark of a tetrahedron is visible on the inner wall.[32] Finally, five sets of tokens belonged to crushed envelopes (table 3). The first group comes from Uruk and consists of fifty-two units,[33]

Table 1. Envelopes Found Complete

	cones	large cones	punched cones	spheres	large spheres	flat disks	lenticular disks	high disks	cylinders	tetrahedrons	large tetrahedrons	punched tetrahedrons	ovoids	incised ovoids	rectangles	triangles	paraboloids	animals	undetermined	TOTAL	Markings
Susa Sb 1927	3	1					3													7	7
Sb 1936					1	1														2	no
Sb 1940							3		3											6	6
Sb 4338					5															5	no
Tepe Yahya	1			2																3	3
TOTAL	4	1		2	6	1	6		3											23	

the second from Chogha Mish yields sixty-one,[34] and finally, three from Susa held respectively fourteen, seven, and four tokens.[35]

X-rays have been used, with unsatisfactory results, to investigate the contents of several specimens from Chogha Mish,[36] Susa,[37] Dharan, and Dumah (table 4). Because the tokens are tightly clustered, they hide one another, making it difficult to take an accurate count. It is impossible to decide with certainty whether a circular shape is to be interpreted as a sphere or a disk. Furthermore, X-ray photographs do not show incised or punched markings.

Tokens Enclosed in Envelopes

The total number of tokens which belonged in envelopes amounts to 345 (table 5). Accordingly, there is an average of 9 tokens per envelope. In reality, however, there are great discrepancies between the number in each of the clay cases: from 2 to 15.

Ten types of tokens were found in envelopes (chart 2). The assemblage is as follows: cones 8.11 percent (28 specimens), spheres 33.62 percent (116), disks 11.59 percent (40), cylinders 16.81 percent (58), tetrahedrons 13.91 percent (48), ovoids 6.66 percent (23), rectangles .29 percent (1), triangles .87 percent (3), paraboloids 2.03 percent (7), animals 1.16 percent (4), and undetermined 4.93 percent (17). There is yet no evidence that biconoids, bent coils, rhomboids, vessels, and tools were stored in envelopes but, of course, this may be because the sample of tokens held in envelopes is so small.

Table 2. Envelopes Found Broken

	cones	large cones	punched cones	spheres	large spheres	flat disks	lenticular disks	high disks	cylinders	tetrahedrons	large tetrahedrons	punched tetrahedrons	ovoids	incised ovoids	rectangles	triangles	paraboloids	animals	undetermined	TOTAL	Markings
Chogha Mish	1			1	1	5														8	no
Farukhabad										1										1	?
Habuba Kabira MII:133														2						2	11
MII:134														6						6	6
Susa Sb 1930				7																7	no
Sb 1938	3			2		1		1									1			8	+
Sb 1942				2																2	no
Sb 1967				4	2					4	3	2								15	no
Sb 5340										2										2	2
Sb 6350							2		2								1	2		7	6
Sb 6946				6																6	no
No Re				1																1	no
S.ACR.I.77 1991.1							3		8											11	no
2049.1									3											3	?
2067.2	1						1													2	no
2089.1				7					3											10	no
2111.2				1					7											8	no
2111.3									6											6	6
2130.1									7											7	7
2130.4				1		1			1											3	no
2142.2									2											2	3
2142.3				3					5											8	8
2173.4			1	4					1											6	6
Uruk W 20987,3				1			1								1					3	no
W 20987,7														7						7	no
W 20987,8					2					5										7	no
W 20987, 15				4	1															5	no
W 20987,17		1		4	1		2		1											9	no
TOTAL	5	1	1	48	3	11	9	1	46	12	3	2		15	1		2	2		162	

Table 3. Groups of Tokens Separated from Envelopes

	cones	large cones	punched cones	spheres	large spheres	flat disks	lenticular disks	high disks	cylinders	tetrahedrons	large tetrahedrons	punched tetrahedrons	ovoids	incised ovoids	rectangles	triangles	paraboloids	animals	undetermined	TOTAL
Susa No. N. ber				8		1			1	3							1			14
ACR 2067.3	3								1											4
ACR 2091.2	1								6											7
Chogha Mish	12			13	2	10				11	8					1			4	61
Uruk W 20987.27				26					1	8	1		5	3		2	4	2		52
TOTAL	16			47	2	11			9	22	9		5	3		3	5	2	4	138

Table 4. Tokens Tentatively Determined by X rays

	cones	large cones	punched cones	spheres	large spheres	flat disks	lenticular disks	high disks	cylinders	tetrahedrons	large tetrahedrons	punched tetrahedrons	ovoids	incised ovoids	rectangles	triangles	paraboloids	animals	undetermined	TOTAL	Markings
Dharan																			10	10	
Dumah																			3	3	
Susa Sb 1932				7	1	1														9?	9
TOTAL				7	1	1													13	22	

Table 5. Totals

	cones	large cones	punched cones	spheres	large spheres	flat disks	lenticular disks	high disks	cylinders	tetrahedrons	large tetrahedrons	punched tetrahedrons	ovoids	incised ovoids	rectangles	triangles	paraboloids	animals	undetermined	TOTAL
Envelopes Found Complete	4	1		2	6	1	6		3											23
Envelopes Found Broken	5	1	1	48	3	11	9	1	46	12	3	2		15	1		2	2		162
Separated Tokens	16			47	2	11			9	22	9		5	3		3	5	2	4	138
Tokens Determined by X rays				7?	1?	1?													13?	22?
TOTAL	25	2	1	104	12	24	15	1	58	34	12	2	5	18	1	3	7	4	17	345

Cones, spheres, and tetrahedrons are featured in two different sizes, small and large; there are flat, lenticular, and high disks; there are examples of incised ovoids and animals and of punched cones and tetrahedrons, bringing the number of token subtypes represented in envelopes to nineteen. Among the nineteen subtypes, twelve are plain subtypes and the remaining seven are complex. The former include cones, large cones, spheres, large spheres, flat disks, lenticular disks, high disks, cylinders, tetrahedrons, large tetrahedrons, ovoids, and rectangles. The latter consist of punched cones, punched tetrahedrons, incised ovoids, triangles, paraboloids, and two types of animal shapes. As a result, among the 345 tokens enclosed in envelopes, 287 are plain, 32 are complex, and 26 are undetermined (including the 22 tokens included in X-rayed envelopes which cannot show markings). In other words, 83.19 percent of the tokens enclosed in envelopes are plain, 9.28 percent are complex, and 7.54 percent are undetermined.

The tokens enclosed in envelopes are identical in types and subtypes to those found loose. Furthermore, the tokens contained in clay cases also occur in different sizes: there are, for example, spheres and large spheres; they bear the same kind of markings, incised or punched. The selection is smaller, probably because the assemblage is also smaller.

Markings

It was a great advantage to have groups of tokens secured in clay cases, often bearing seals of authority. Most envelopes are covered with seal im-

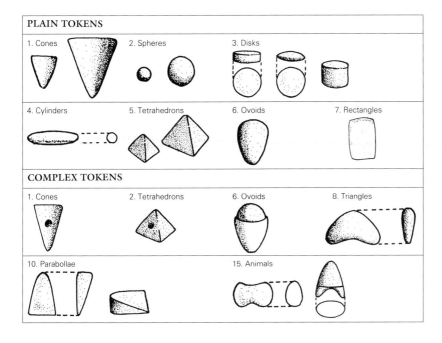

Chart 2. Tokens
included in envelopes.

Fig. 13. Envelope covered with one cylinder seal impression, Susa (Sb 1935), Iran. Courtesy Musée du Louvre, Département des Antiquités Orientales.

pressions. As a rule, a single cylinder seal was impressed all over the artifact (fig. 13), but there are instances when two or three different seals were used. The major drawback of the envelopes was that they concealed the counters: once the tokens were enclosed, they were no longer visible. While the string of tokens could be checked at all times, it was not possible to verify the contents of an envelope without breaking it and, therefore, without tampering with the sealings. It was probably to overcome this difficulty that systems of markings were developed. The term *marking* is used to refer to notations on envelopes, *sign* for notations on tablets.

Before proceeding to the description of these various markings, it should be emphasized that the total number of marked specimens amounts to only nineteen specimens, or 9 percent of the total number of artifacts. Envelopes bearing markings are now attested in three sites: Susa, Habuba Kabira, and Tepe Yahya. The rarity of envelopes bearing markings can perhaps be attributed to excavation luck; otherwise, it seems to indicate that the usage was not widespread.

One method of showing what was inside the envelopes consisted of attaching a set of tokens, presumably identical to those enclosed, onto the outer surface of the case. This was done by sinking the counters in the clay when it was still soft. This method is represented by a single fragment from Susa, displaying two plain cylinders embedded in the surface (fig. 14).[38] The fact that only one example was recovered suggests that the method was not widely used.

Fourteen envelopes, including twelve at Susa[39] and two at Habuba Kabira, bore markings impressed into their surface when the clay was still soft. In this technique, the markings were shown in one-to-one correspondence;

that is, each token enclosed was indicated by one marking on the surface of the case. For example, an envelope holding six tokens displayed six markings. This is supported by the fact that all the envelopes of this category, recovered intact, have a number of markings equal to the number of tokens enclosed. In other words, only broken envelopes show a discrepancy between the number of markings and the number of associated tokens.

The markings indicated not only the number of tokens included but also the shape of each counter. For example, Susa Sb 1940 yielded three lenticular disks and three cylinders which were shown by three circular and three long markings (fig. 15). Nine subtypes of tokens were represented in the thirteen envelopes bearing impressed markings. These include small, large, and punched cones, spheres, lenticular disks, cylinders, incised ovoids and, perhaps, parabolas and animal shapes. Examination of the markings shows that little systematization was used to depict the various tokens, except for spheres and disks. These were translated by different circular markings: the former took the shape of a deep punch, whereas the latter was a wide, shallow depression. Cones were impressed in several ways, either in profile,[40] with the tip,[41] or with the base.[42] In this last instance, the token represented was a large punched cone, which was thus shown by a shallow circular marking of an even greater diameter than that of a lenticular disk. The cylinders appear as long wedges. The incised ovoids were shown by an oval impression with a small ridge left by the incision at the maximum diameter.

There were several ways of impressing the markings in the soft clay. The

Fig. 14. Envelope with a set of tokens sunk into the surface, Susa (Sb 5340), Iran. Courtesy Musée du Louvre, Département des Antiquités Orientales.

Fig. 15. Envelope
bearing impressed
markings corresponding
to the tokens held
inside, Susa (Sb 1940),
Iran. Courtesy Musée
du Louvre, Départe-
ment des Antiquités
Orientales.

most direct, illustrated by M II: 134 of Habuba Kabira, was to press the
tokens against the surface of the envelope before enclosing them inside.
There can be no doubt about this technique, because the incised ovoids,
found associated with the Habuba Kabira envelope, fit perfectly in the oval
cavities left in the clay case about fifty-five hundred years ago (fig. 16). It is
tempting to speculate that the method of embedding actual tokens into the
surface of envelopes led to the method of showing their negative imprint.
The second envelope of Habuba Kabira and most examples from Susa ex-
hibited yet another method of conveying the information. In these cases,
the markings were not stamped with tokens but were impressed with a stick
or stylus.[43] Finally, traces of fingernails(?) on circular impressions of a Susa
envelope suggest that they may have been done with the thumb.[44]

Another technique consisted of marking the envelopes when the clay
was already dry (perhaps as an afterthought?). Consequently, the markings
were scratched rather than impressed, making it more difficult to render the
shape of the counters. In both specimens of this category the number of
markings matched the tokens but their shape did not. In the first example,
which comes from Tepe Yahya, there is little difference between three signs
meant to represent two spheres and a cone (fig. 17). In the second specimen,
from Susa, no effort was made to match the shapes of six spheres, which
were simply indicated by six strokes, whereas a large sphere and flat disk
were shown, apparently, by a circular and a triangular punch mark.[45]

Seven specimens, again from Susa, were punctured through the thickness of the wall at diametrical ends.[46] The perforations have been interpreted by some as a means of preventing the artifacts from breaking while
firing.[47] It is more likely, however, that the perforations allowed the passage
of a string holding a number of tokens duplicating the set inside. The per-

Fig. 16. Envelope
bearing the impression
of incised ovoids,
Habuba Kabira (M II:
134), Syria. Photo by
Klaus Anger; courtesy
Museum für Vor- und
Frühgeschichte, Berlin.

Fig. 17. Envelope
bearing three markings,
scratched in after the
clay had dried, Tepe
Yahya, Iran. Courtesy
Peabody Museum,
Harvard University.

forated envelopes can be considered, therefore, as yet another possible technique for indicating the contents of envelopes.

In all cases except one, the information communicated by the markings on the envelopes pertained to the number and types of the tokens enclosed. A unique envelope of Susa, marked with a cross, shows on the X-ray photograph a yield of eight tokens.[48] In this case, the sign apparently did not communicate the number or the shape of the tokens inside. Instead, the information concerned, perhaps, the nature of the transaction. Alternatively, the marking could be an accountant's colophon.

IT IS INTERESTING that many techniques were devised for showing the token contents of envelopes: (1) attaching tokens to the surface; (2) stamping the tokens in the soft clay; (3) impressing signs with a stick or stylus; (4) pressing with the thumb; (5) scratching the clay when hard; and (6?) securing by a string. Most proved to be dead ends and disappeared. But token impressions and markings inscribed with a blunt stylus were carried over to the first tablets. They were the beginning of writing. Envelopes, which started as an accessory to the token system, came to transform it in the most unexpected way. They triggered the mutation of the three-dimensional tokens into two-dimensional graphic symbols. This unique event was to have important consequences for communication.

Impressed Tablets

And when we consider the first uses to which writing was put, it would seem quite clear that it was connected first and foremost with power: it was used for inventories, catalogues, censuses, laws and instructions; in all instances, whether the aim was to keep a check on material possessions or on human beings, it is evidence of the power exercised by some men over other men and over worldly possessions.

— CLAUDE LÉVI-STRAUSS[1]

THE SYSTEM OF MARKINGS on clay envelopes ushered in a new phase of the token system. At first, the impressed notations were ancillary to the counters, but eventually they supplanted them. This occurred when solid clay tablets bearing impressed signs replaced the hollow envelopes holding tokens. These impressed signs still perpetuated the shape of the tokens, but they assumed an entirely new function. Whereas the markings on envelopes repeated only the message encoded in the tokens held within, the signs impressed on tablets *were* the message. The first tablets were a decisive step in the invention of writing and amounted to a revolution in communication technology. This chapter deals with the earliest tablets bearing signs in the shape of tokens. I will document the number of these artifacts recovered and recount their geographic distribution (map 3), context, and chronology. I will describe the tablets and the signs they bear. Most important, I will trace the evolution from tokens to markings on envelopes and impressed signs on tablets. Finally, I will show that impressed signs are the immediate forerunners of the Sumerian pictographic script.

NUMBER

The total number of impressed tablets, complete or fragmentary, included in the present study amounts to about 240. The majority, some 150 specimens, come from Iran. The 90 tablets from Susa have been recovered in successive excavation campaigns from 1912 to 1977.[2] Forty-two specimens were excavated in Godin Tepe,[3] 13 from Sialk,[4] and 1 from Tall-i-Ghazir.[5] Six of an undisclosed number of impressed tablets are published for Chogha Mish.[6] The number of Iraqi examples is about 67. Information is available on 65 impressed tablets from Uruk.[7] There is a single specimen from Khafaje[8] and a fragment from Nineveh.[9] There are 25 tablets from Syria, with 10 coming from Habuba Kabira,[10] 13 from Jebel Aruda,[11] 1 from Tell Brak,[12] and 1 from Mari.[13]

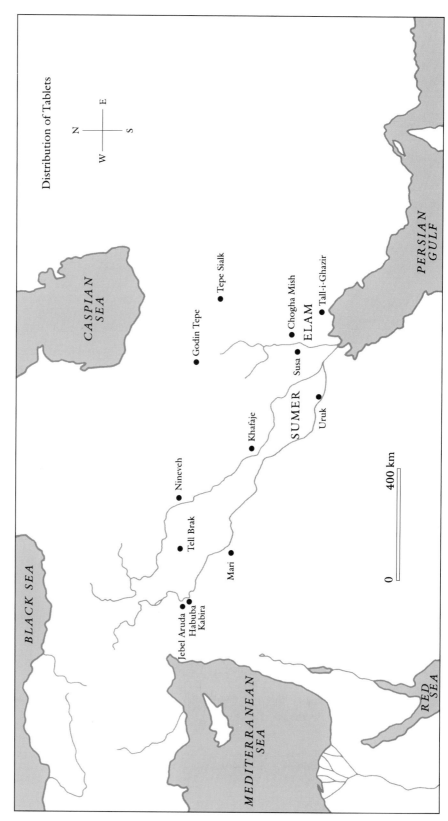

Map 3. Distribution of tablets.

In the sites yielding impressed tablets as well as envelopes, the two kinds of artifacts are found in the same context. At Susa, tablets and envelopes were located in the same area of the Acropolis, in some cases in the same building and the same room and, in one instance, even in the same container.[14] Building 2 of Habuba Kabira produced impressed tablets as well as envelopes.[15] Forty tablets from Uruk belonged to the sanctuary of Eanna, as did twenty-five envelopes. An additional twenty were discovered in the Anu Ziggurat, the second major sanctuary of Uruk, where so far no envelopes have been uncovered. Several of these tablets lay *in situ* on the floor of the White Temple.[16]

As a rule the impressed tablets were located, like the envelopes, in temple precincts and administrative buildings. At Godin Tepe, the largest cache of tablets came from the gate house at the entrance of the compound, and a second group came from an imposing building probably used for official functions.[17]

CHRONOLOGY

The impressed tablets can be divided into three closely consecutive groups, ranging from about 3500 to 3000 B.C. The first group, dated to ca. 3500 B.C., includes the impressed tablets of Susa 18 and Habuba Kabira. Some of the tablets from Eanna and Chogha Mish might also belong to the period of Uruk VI.

The tablets of Susa 17 date between 3300 and 3100 B.C. They are contemporaneous with the twenty-nine tablets of the Red Temple of Uruk and with those of the Anu Ziggurat in Uruk IVa.[18] The forty-three tablets of Godin Tepe, including one specimen bearing an incised sign, may be included in this second group,[19] together with those from Jebel Aruda, whose carbon 14 dates cluster around 3200 B.C.[20]

The tablets of Sialk and Tall-i-Ghazir, associated with high beveled-rim bowls (*Blumentopf*), Proto-Elamite sealings, and lugged jars with rope appliqué bands, belong to the third group, estimated to Uruk III and Susa 16, or about 3100 to 3000 B.C. The seal impression on the Nineveh tablet suggests a similar date, although it has been assigned to level V, dated to 2900–2500 B.C.[21]

The chronology of the impressed tablet is important because it clearly demonstrates that impressed signs preceded pictography by an interval of about two hundred years, or some eight generations. There are no pictographic texts contemporaneous with the earliest group of impressed tablets from Susa 18 and Uruk VI–IVc. The earliest evidence of pictography consists of a group of tablets recovered on the floor of Temple C, in Uruk Oc XVI 3: "On the floor, under the collapsed roof of Temple C's T-shaped hall, in level IVa." These seven tablets may be as early as Uruk IVb[22] or as late as IVa.[23] Consequently, it is about 3300–3100 B.C., during the period of the second group of impressed tablets, that the two kinds of writing began to coexist. This is illustrated at Godin Tepe[24] and at Sialk, where the two types of tablets were found together.[25]

DESCRIPTION

All the impressed tablets were made of clay, except for twenty-two plaster specimens recovered in the Anu Ziggurat of Uruk.[26] The tablets are small, fitting comfortably in the palm of the hand. On average, they are about 5 cm wide, 4 cm long, and 2 cm thick. They are modeled in various shapes, with the lack of standardization typical of a new craft. A number are oval, some roundish, others square or rectangular. The profile of the tablets is also highly variable, and while most specimens are convex, some are flat and still others are plano-convex. Many of these documents were authenticated by seals. The seal impressions cover the impressed signs, showing that the tablets were first inscribed and then sealed.

THE SIGNS

For the sake of clarity, I call the notations on tablets *signs,* whereas those on envelopes are referred to as *markings.* Seventeen signs can be identified on the impressed tablets.

1. SHORT WEDGE
   A. small (fig. 18)
   B. large (fig. 19)
   C. punched (fig. 20)
   D. sideways
   E. apex to apex (fig. 21)

Fig. 18. Tablet showing a line of four circular signs followed by a line of four short wedges, Godin Tepe (Gd 73–19), Iran. Courtesy T. Cuyler Young, Jr.

Fig. 19. Tablet with
three large wedges,
one shallow circular
marking, and four
deep circular markings,
Susa (Sb 2313), Iran.
Courtesy Musée du
Louvre, Département
des Antiquités
Orientales.

Fig. 20. Unlisted sign
similar to a token in the
shape of a cylinder with
all-over strokes (type 4:
10/11), Uruk (W 20973),
Iraq. Courtesy
Deutsches Archaeo-
logisches Institut,
Abteilung Baghdad.

2. DEEP CIRCULAR

A. small (fig. 18)
B. large
C. semicircular
D. incised (fig. 22)
E. punched
F. appendix

Fig. 21. Tablet with five short wedges, two triangular signs, and one apex-to-apex sign, Godin Tepe (Gd 73–291), Iran. Courtesy T. Cuyler Young, Jr.

Fig. 22. Impressed tablet with deep circular incised and triangular incised signs, Susa (Sb 1975 bis), Iran. Courtesy Musée du Louvre, Département des Antiquités Orientales. Drawing by Ellen Simmons. (The tablet is shown upside down.)

Fig. 23. Impressed tablet, long wedges, Susa (Sb 6291), Iran. Courtesy Musée du Louvre, Département des Antiquités Orientales.

3. SHALLOW CIRCULAR

A. lenticular

B. flat (fig. 19)

4. LONG WEDGE (fig. 23)

5. OVAL

6. TRIANGULAR

A. plain

B. incised (fig. 22)

The Layout

Most tablets are inscribed on the obverse only, but some bear additional notations on the reverse or along the edges.[27] In the latter two cases, each face presents a separate account, and in no instance does the reverse indicate a total, as is the case in later pictographic tablets. Some tablets were turned like the page of a book to read the second face,[28] but others were turned on a horizontal axis.[29]

The signs are normally organized in horizontal lines parallel to the longer side of the tablet. Signs of different types are usually not mixed within the same line. Instead, each line consists of identical signs. For example, a line of circular signs is followed by a line of wedges (fig. 18). When there are only a few signs in a line, they are placed in the center, rather than to the side. The signs are by no means randomly aligned but are organized in hierarchical order. The largest units, placed at the top of the tablets, are followed by lines of signs of decreasing value. For example, a line of circular signs standing for large measures of grain precedes a line of wedges, which, as will be shown later, represented smaller units of grain (fig. 18).

Because each line consisted of series of identical signs, the tablets could

Fig. 24. Impressed
tablet, boustrophedon,
Godin Tepe (Gd 73–
292), Iran. Courtesy
T. Cuyler Young, Jr.

be read in any direction. Several specimens indicate, however, that writing usually proceeded from top to bottom and from right to left and perhaps continued in the opposite direction (boustrophedon). Among these examples, a tablet from Godin Tepe has a complete line of signs in the upper part of the tablet and the two last units are added below (fig. 24).[30] Sb 2313 from Susa illustrates how, on the few occasions when a line is composed of different signs, the larger units were at the right, followed by lesser units toward the left. Since the scribes placed the signs in hierarchical order, starting with the largest units, we may logically deduce that the signs on the right were written before those on the left (fig. 19). Finally, tablet 73–292 of Godin Tepe has a line starting from the right and a second line starting from the left, or boustrophedon (fig. 24).[31]

The Technique of Impression

The techniques for impressing signs on tablets were the same as those used for envelopes. Signs were still made by pressing tokens against the surface of the tablets. This is visibly the case for Sb 2313 of Susa (fig. 19), which bears three large wedges showing distinctly the entire outline of the cone used for impressing them. The signs corresponding to pinched spheres, biconoids, ovoids, and triangles had to be impressed with tokens since no stylus could have achieved such shapes. In other cases, circular signs and wedges were impressed with a blunt stylus.

Some signs can be described as representing a mixed impressed/incised technique (signs 2d and 6b above). On Sb 1975 bis from Susa, a token triangle was impressed four times on the face of the tablet, and each of these triangular impressions was completed by a vertical incision performed with a pointed stylus (fig. 22), reproducing a triangle with an incised line (type 8: 11).

Each of the seventeen impressed signs can be traced to a token proto-type. Considering the limited sampling of nineteen marked envelopes and 240 tablets, it is remarkable that in seven instances the development from tokens to markings on envelopes and signs on tablets can be fully documented. The relevant information will be presented below, as follows:

A. A type of token found at large.
B. The same token enclosed in an unmarked envelope.
C. The corresponding marking on the surface of an envelope.
D. The matching sign impressed on a tablet.
E. The occurrence on a pictographic tablet as an impressed sign, an incised pictograph, or an impressed/incised sign.
F. The proposed translation.

A complete list of all the artifacts involved will not be given. Where possible, a tentative interpretation of the signs will be provided. These interpretations correspond to those of M. W. Green and Hans J. Nissen,[32] Hans J. Nissen, Peter Damerow, and Robert K. Englund,[33] Adam Falkenstein,[34] Jöran Friberg,[35] or A. A. Vaiman.[36] It should be understood that the Sumerian standardized units which these authors are citing reflect the highly organized city-state society of the late fourth to early third millennia. The meaning of the signs and of their prehistoric token prototypes will be discussed in the concluding section of this chapter.

1a. SHORT WEDGE

A. Cone, type 1: 1.
B. Unmarked envelope: Chogha Mish,[37] Susa.[38]
C. Marking on envelope: Tepe Yahya (fig. 17),[39] Susa.[40]
D. Impressed sign: Chogha Mish,[41] Godin Tepe,[42] Jebel Aruda,[43] Khafaje,[44] Sialk,[45] Susa,[46] Uruk.[47]
E. ATU 892/ZATU N-1 (impressed).
F. Measure of grain (1 *ban*?).[48]

Comment: On the envelope Sb 1927, from Susa, cones were represented by pressing the tips of the counters into the clay, rather than pressing the complete counter sideways, thus resulting in mostly circular markings.[49] This same technique was perhaps perpetuated on one tablet of Susa.[50]

1b. LARGE WEDGE

A. Large cone, type 1: 2.
B. Unmarked envelope: Chogha Mish.[51]
C. Marking on envelope: Susa.[52]
D. Impressed sign: Jebel Aruda,[53] Susa (fig. 19).[54]

E. ATU 899/ZATU N-34 (impressed).

F. Measure of grain (180 *ban?*).[55]

1c. PUNCHED WEDGE

A. Punched cone, type 1: 19.

B. Unmarked envelope: None.

C. Marking on envelope: Susa.[56]

D. Impressed sign: Uruk (fig. 20).

E. ATU 905/ZATU N-48 (impressed).

F. Measure of grain (1,800 *ban?*).[57]
Unit of land measure (1 *ešé?*).[58]

Comment: The only punched cone enclosed in an envelope was translated by the impression of its base, leaving a large circular marking rather than a punched wedge.

1d. HORIZONTAL WEDGE

A. Cone, type 1: 1.

D. Impressed sign: Godin Tepe.[59]

E. ATU 918 (impressed).

F. Fraction.[60]
Unit of land measure (1/4 *iku?*).[61]

1e. TWO WEDGES APEX TO APEX

A. Cone, type 1: 1

D. Impressed sign: Godin Tepe (fig. 21).[62]

E. ATU 918 (impressed).

F. Measure of grain (1/10 *ban?*).[63]

2a. CIRCULAR SIGN

A. Sphere, type 2: 1.

B. Unmarked envelope: Chogha Mish,[64] Susa,[65] Uruk.[66]

C. Marking on envelope: Susa,[67] Tepe Yahya.[68]

D. Impressed sign: Godin Tepe,[69] Jebel Aruda,[70] Habuba Kabira,[71] Khafaje,[72] Nineveh,[73] Sialk,[74] Susa,[75] Uruk.[76]

E. ATU 897/ZATU N-14 (impressed).

F. Unit of grain (1 *bariga?*).[77]

Comment: In one instance an envelope holding six spheres showed six strokes on the outside.[78] The markings were scratched when the clay had already hardened and when it was no longer possible to impress the tokens.

2b. LARGE CIRCULAR SIGN

A. Large sphere, type 2: 2.

B. Enclosed in unmarked envelope: Chogha Mish,[79] Susa.[80]

C. Marking on envelope: None.
D. Impressed sign: Susa,[81] Habuba Kabira,[82] Jebel Aruda.[83]
E. ATU 913/ZATU N-45 (impressed).
F. Unit of grain metrology (10 *bariga?*).[84]

Comment: None of the envelopes containing large spheres featured markings. It can only be presumed that large spheres came to be represented by deep circular markings, larger than those standing for small spheres. This hypothesis is supported by impressed tablets, such as those of Habuba Kabira, showing the existence of deep circular markings of different sizes and organized in separate lines.[85]

2c. SEMI-CIRCULAR

A. Half sphere, type 2: 24.
B. Unmarked envelope: None.
C. Marking on envelope: None.
D. Impressed sign: Godin Tepe,[86] Sialk.[87]

Comment: The half sphere is one of the earliest token subtypes; it is found in many assemblages but never occurs in large numbers. This explains, perhaps, why none has ever been recovered in an envelope and why the corresponding sign is also infrequently used on tablets.

2d. CIRCULAR SIGN WITH ONE INCISION

A. Notched sphere, type 2: 7.
B. Unmarked envelope: None.
C. Marking on envelope: None.
D. Impressed sign: Susa (fig. 22).[88]
E. ATU 898/ZATU N-15 (impressed).
F. Measure of grain(?) (1 *bariga?*).[89]
Unit of land measure (1/8 *iku?*).[90]

2e. PUNCHED CIRCULAR SIGN

A. Punched sphere, type 2: 3.
B. Unmarked envelope: None.
C. Marking on envelope: None.
D. Impressed tablet: Tall-i-Ghazir.[91]
E. ZATU N-50 (impressed).
F. Unit of land measure (10 *bur?*).[92]

2f. CIRCULAR WITH AN APPENDIX

A. Pinched sphere, type 2: 15.
B. Unmarked envelope: None.
C. Marking on envelope: None.
D. Impressed sign: Susa.[93]

E. ATU 781/ZATU 240 (incised).

F. Fat-tailed sheep.

Comment: The sign ATU 781/ZATU 240 shares the same outline but bears an additional incised cross.

3a. SHALLOW CIRCULAR MARKING

A. Flat disk, type 3: 1.

B. Unmarked envelope: Chogha Mish,[94] Susa,[95] Uruk.[96]

C. Marking on envelope: None.

D. Impressed sign: Susa.[97]

E. ATU 907 (impressed).

F. Unit of grain metrology(?).[98]

Comment: Lenticular disks (type 3: 3) are represented by shallow circular markings on two envelopes from Susa.[99] However, none of the envelopes containing flat disks bears markings. It can only be hypothesized that they too were represented by large shallow circular markings showing, probably, a more defined outline than the lenticular disks. The value of the flat disk may be hypothesized from the tokens with which they are associated. It is probably meaningful that in four instances when disks with straight edges were included in envelopes, they were associated with small spheres[100] or with small and large spheres.[101] The association of spheres and flat disks in envelopes seems to correspond with the association of deep and shallow circular impressed signs on tablets.[102]

3b. CIRCULAR SIGN DERIVING FROM THE LENTICULAR DISK

A. Lenticular disk, type 3: 10.

B. Unmarked envelope: Susa.[103]

C. Marking on envelope: Susa (fig. 15).[104]

D. Impressed sign: Chogha Mish,[105] Jebel Aruda,[106] Susa,[107] Tell Brak,[108] Uruk.[109]

F. Unit of animal numeration (10 animals?).[110]

Comment: Lenticular disks held in envelopes were mostly associated with cylinders.[111] When these two kinds of tokens are translated into markings, they appear as shallow circular markings and long wedges. Accordingly, I presume that when circular signs are associated on a tablet with long wedges, they can be understood as deriving from the lenticular disk.[112]

4. LONG WEDGE

A. Cylinder, type 4: 1.

B. Unmarked envelope: Susa,[113] Uruk.[114]

C. Markings on envelope: Susa (fig. 15).[115]

D. Impressed sign: Godin Tepe,[116] Habuba Kabira,[117] Jebel Aruda,[118] Susa (fig. 23),[119] Tell Brak,[120] Uruk.[121]

F. Unit of animal numeration (1 animal?).[122]

5a. OVAL

A. Ovoid, type 6: 1.

B. Unmarked envelope: Uruk.[123]

C. Marking on envelope: None.

D. Impressed sign: Chogha Mish,[124] Habuba Kabira,[125] Jebel Aruda.[126]

5b. INCISED OVOID

A. Ovoid with an incised circular line, type 6: 14.

B. Unmarked envelope: Uruk (fig. 12).[127]

C. Marking on envelope: Habuba Kabira (fig. 16).[128]

D. Impressed sign: None.

E. ATU 733/ZATU 393.

F. Oil.

Comment: The incised ovoid is included here even though it is not represented on an impressed tablet but only as a marking on an envelope. On the envelope M II: 134, from Habuba Kabira, it is clear that the markings were made by impressing the counters into the clay wall, for the resulting oval impressions show a small ridge corresponding to the incision on the token. There is conflicting information concerning M II: 133. In this case, the markings may be simple wedges done with a stylus.

6a. PLAIN TRIANGULAR

A. Triangle, type 8: 2.

B. Enclosed in unmarked envelope: Uruk,[129] Chogha Mish.[130]

C. Marking on envelope: None.

D. Impressed sign: Godin Tepe (fig. 21).[131]

E. ATU 935/ZATU N-39a (impressed).

F. Measure of grain (1/5 *ban*?).[132]

6b. INCISED TRIANGULAR

A. Triangle with a median incised line, type 8: 11.

B. Unmarked envelope: None.

C. Marking on envelope: None.

D. Impressed sign: Susa (fig. 22).[133]

E. Impressed/incised sign: Susa.[134]

F. Unit of wheat(?)[135]

BEYOND THE IMPRESSED TABLETS: PICTOGRAPHY

The documentation presented above shows that the impressed tablets represented only a transitional phase of writing leading to pictography—in this case, the graphic representation of tokens. The chart on pages 69–70 illustrates how some of the impressed signs were supplanted by pictographs traced with a sharp stylus. For example, oval and triangular signs evolved into incised pictographs, while still other signs became impressed/incised. On the other hand, wedges and circular signs remained impressed, creating a dichotomy between two kinds of scripts: impressed and pictographic. In the following section, I will discuss how the emergence of two different scripts may be explained by the two kinds of prototypes: plain and complex tokens.

The Tokens as Prototypes of Impressed Signs

The most common types of tokens, which pervaded the entire Near East— cones, spheres, disks, and cylinders—gave rise to the most common impressed signs. These counters, including punched cones and spheres, are also among the most ancient token shapes, occurring among the earliest assemblages of Tepe Asiab and Ganj Dareh Tepe and persisting without discontinuity until the fourth millennium B.C.

Perhaps most significant, cones, punched cones, spheres, disks, and cylinders are among the subtypes most frequently held in envelopes and, subsequently, most commonly translated into impressed markings on the surface of envelopes. This suggests that the fashion in which tokens were kept in archives determined the resulting script.

Sign impression was the most ancient and also the most rudimentary of the two early forms of writing. The major drawback of the impressed technique was the blurring of the shapes of the token prototypes. For example, tokens of distinctive forms—such as cones and cylinders, or disks and spheres—were transcribed, respectively, into closely related wedges or circular signs. As a result, the signs were identified by context rather than by shape. Thus, short and long wedges representing cones and cylinders were distinguished by their position on the tablet: the long wedges were systematically placed near the edge of a tablet,[136] whereas the short wedges were traced at the center of the field.[137] The circular signs deriving from spheres and lenticular disks could be set apart by their association with other signs. Those standing for spheres were combined with short wedges,[138] those representing lenticular disks were combined with long wedges.[139]

The Tokens as Prototypes of Impressed/Incised Signs

Notched spheres (type 2: 7)[140] and incised triangles (type 8: 11) were the prototypes for impressed/incised signs. These signs are very important because they attest to the close relationship between impressed and incised signs. They show, beyond any doubt, that the incised pictographs came

Sign	Token	Enclosed in envelope	Marking on envelope	Sign impressed on tablet	Incised pictograph

x signifies occurrence; a blank signifies no evidence

Sign	Token	Enclosed in envelope	Marking on envelope	Sign impressed on tablet	Incised pictograph
1.a		x	x		
1.b		x	x		
1.c		x	x		
1.d					
1.e	x				
2.a		x	x		
2.b		x			
2.c					
2.d					

Sign	Token	Enclosed in envelope	Marking on envelope	Sign impressed on tablet	Incised pictograph

x signifies occurrence; a blank signifies no evidence

2.e					x
2.f					x
3.a		x			
3.b		x	x		
4		x	x		
5.a		x			x
5.b		x	x		
6.a		x			x
6.b		x	x		x

as the third and final step of the evolution from tokens to writing. The incised triangle is of particular interest since one can trace it through the following four stages of evolution: (1) complex token, (2) impressed sign, (3) impressed/incised sign, and (4) pictograph. Although the incised triangles were among the more frequent subtypes of fourth-millennium complex tokens, none so far has been found enclosed in an envelope. Impressions of incised triangles occur on the "solid clay ball" of Susa.[141] The impressed/incised sign that followed consisted in complementing a triangular token impression with an incised marking (fig. 22).[142] Finally came the pictograph ATU 900.

The Tokens as Prototypes of Incised Pictographs

Four more impressed signs/markings evolved into incised pictographs. The technique was not new: tokens had been marked by incised lines as early as the beginning of the system in the eighth millennium B.C., and incised markings became especially important with the complex tokens of the fourth millennium. However, the use of a stylus to trace signs on a tablet followed the impressed script, constituting a third stage in the evolution of writing in the Near East (after markings on envelopes and impressed signs). The resulting incised signs had the advantage of being far more legible than those which were impressed. The incised signs represented with greater accuracy the profile of the token prototypes, as well as the markings displayed on their surface. This was an important feature because the pictographs derived mostly from complex tokens characterized by linear markings.

Among the impressed markings which evolved into pictographs, the incised ovoids (type 6: 14) are most important because they can be traced at each of the four steps of the evolution. First, incised ovoids were among the most common complex tokens in fourth-millennium sites; second, they were held in unmarked envelopes at Uruk;[143] third, they appear as impressed markings on an envelope from Habuba Kabira;[144] and fourth, they become the incised pictograph ATU 733/ZATU 293. There is, however, no known corresponding impressed sign.

The three remaining token subtypes perpetuated both by impressed signs and pictographs include pinched spheres (type 2: 15), plain ovoids (type 6: 1), and plain triangles (type 8: 2). These tokens can be matched to ATU 781/ZATU 240,[145] ATU 732/ZATU 280, 709, and ATU 428/ZATU 254. All these tokens are typically complex and, except for the plain ovoids, are never part of assemblages prior to the middle of the fourth millennium B.C.

The last and most important category of complex tokens that contributed to the Sumerian pictographic script has thus far not been identified in envelopes. That is perhaps because so few envelopes are known, but more likely it is because, as I have discussed in the previous chapter, complex tokens were often perforated and therefore were probably attached by a string when they were held in archives. Their listing includes the examples in the chart on pages 72–78.

	Token Type		Pictograph	Translation
				1. Animals
	3: 14		ATU 803 ZATU 482c	lamb
	3: 51		ATU 761 ZATU 575	sheep (fig. 25)
	3: 54		ATU 763 ZATU 571	ewe
	14: 3		ATU 45a ZATU 12	cow
	14: 8		ATU 30 ZATU 145	dog

Fig. 25. Sign ATU 761/ ZATU 575, "sheep," Uruk (W 21418.4), Iraq. Courtesy Deutsches Archaeologisches Institut, Abteilung Baghdad.

Token Type	Pictograph	Translation
		2. Foods
1: 29	ATU 535 ZATU 196	bread
6: 14	ATU 733 ZATU 393	oil
8: 29	ATU 539 ZATU 197	food
9: 1	ATU 428 ZATU 254	sweet (honey?)
9: 15	ATU 750 ZATU 503	sweet (honey?)
13: 3	ATU 139 ZATU 88b	beer[146]
13: 7	ATU 158 ZATU 296a	sheep's milk
		3. Textiles
3: 20	ATU 758 ZATU 452b	textile[147]
3: 21	ATU 798 ZATU 452b	wool[148]

	Token Type		Pictograph	Translation
	3: 22		ZATU 452c	type of garment or cloth
	3: 24		ZATU 452b	type of garment or cloth[149]
	3: 28		ATU 755 ZATU 555	type of garment or cloth[150]
	3: 30		ATU 759 ZATU 452e	type of garment or cloth[151]
	3: 32		ZATU 452e	type of garment or cloth (fig. 26)[152]

Fig. 26. Sign ZATU 452e, "textile," Uruk (W 9657), Iraq. Courtesy Deutsches Archaeologisches Institut, Abteilung Baghdad.

	Token Type		Pictograph	Translation
	3: 52			type of garment or cloth[153]
	3: 55		PI 385 ZATU 452a	wool, fleece[154]
	4: 23		ATU 508	rope
	7: 18		ATU 589 ZATU 764	type of mat or rug
	10: 4		ATU 390/829 ZATU 662/663	type of garment or cloth[155]
	10: 9			type of garment or cloth[156]
	10: 12		PI 158	type of garment or cloth[157]
	10: 13		ATU 685 ZATU 644	type of garment or cloth[158]
	1: 34		ATU 736 ZATU 394	

4. Types of Containers

?

	Token Type		Pictograph	Translation
	7: 31		ATU 568 ZATU 616	granary
	13: 6		ATU 674 ZATU 126	?
				5. Commodities
	1: 38, 39		ZATU 267	perfume
	8: 14		ZATU 63	metal
	8: 15		ATU 545	metal
	8: 17		ATU 703 ZATU 301	metal
	8: 18		ATU 545 ZATU 63	metal
	9: 13		ZATU 293	bracelet, ring
	14: 10		ZATU 379	bed

Token Type	Pictograph	Translation
		6. Service/Work
5: 1	ATU 526 ZATU 280	make, build
		7. Miscellaneous
1: 33	ZATU N 38	number(?)
2: 15	unrecorded	(W 21090)
3: 19	ATU 754 ZATU 127	?
4: 20	ZATU 779	?
4: 24	unrecorded	(W 20973) (fig. 20)
5: 1	ATU 403 ZATU 659	?
5: 5	ATU 406 ZATU 661	?

	Token Type		Pictograph	Translation
	6: 1		ATU 732 ZATU 280	nail(?)
	7: 12		ATU 559	?
	8: 1		ATU 709	?
	8: 37		ATU 712 ZATU 83	?
	9: 6		ATU 434	?
	9: 7		ATU 434	?
	9: 10		ATU 429 ZATU 293(?)	?
	16: 6		ATU 17 ZATU 82	foot

Comment: The meaning of tetrahedrons remains enigmatic. They are among the plain tokens which are both consistently found at large and most frequently included in envelopes. It is to be expected, therefore, that they were perpetuated in writing. However, none of the envelopes that hold tetrahedrons bears impressed markings; nor do we yet have an impressed tablet with triangular impressions.

It is possible that the tetrahedron represented a docket or unit of work.[159] The tetrahedron correlates with the two triangular signs ATU 403/ZATU 659, identified by René Labat as *lagar* ("temple servant"),[160] or to ATU 526/ZATU 280, KAK (du3), traditionally interpreted as "make, build." Clay dockets in the shape of tetrahedrons were used, for example, at Sippar in the third and second millennia B.C.[161] The date and name of individuals written on the dockets make it clear that the objects were meant to be exchanged against rations of barley as wages. Perhaps these late dockets perpetuated both the shape and the meaning of the prehistoric tokens. This idea seems plausible, for manpower was an important commodity of exchange in the ancient Near East. This is attested by the numerous texts referring to workmen digging canals, constructing buildings, and harvesting fields.

If the tetrahedrons truly represent a unit of work, it would be logical to assume that the various sizes of the tokens expressed time units such as one day's work (or one week's or one month's), unless they referred to different salary rates according to the size of a team or the kind of labor.

IN SUM, certain tokens, mostly plain, were perpetuated by impressed signs while others, mostly complex, were transcribed into incised pictographs. It is evident that complex tokens, characterized by multiple markings, did not lend themselves to being impressed and were more conveniently translated by signs traced with a stylus. However, the reason why two different styles of script developed may lie in the way tokens were handled in various offices. Cones, punched cones, spheres, disks, and cylinders were mostly kept in envelopes — and therefore came to be translated by impressed markings. On the other hand, complex tokens were perforated and strung and thus were never transcribed into impressed markings. In turn, the different ways of keeping tokens in archives may be explained by the sort of goods each type of token represented. The plain tokens represented products of the farm and the countryside, whereas complex tokens stood for goods manufactured in the city. It is therefore logical to assume that the two types of tokens were handled by different hands in different offices. It is noteworthy that the incised ovoids were exceptional in being sometimes kept in envelopes and sometimes perforated in order to be strung. At Uruk, for example, in the collection of thirty incised ovoids, ten were held in envelopes (fig. 12)[162] and five[163] were perforated. This may explain why the incised ovoids were transcribed both into impressed and incised signs.

THE MEANING OF SIGNS AND THEIR CORRESPONDING TOKENS

The key to understanding the meaning of pictographs, impressed markings and, ultimately, tokens lies in the cuneiform script of the third millennium B.C. Assyriologists can, in some instances, trace the evolution of cuneiform characters backward through more and more archaic forms to their proto- types in the late fourth millennium B.C. The interpretation of pictographs and impressed signs proposed here is the outcome of such research by A. Falkenstein, M. W. Green, S. Langdon, K. Szarzynska, and A. A. Vaiman, all of whom assumed that, logically, the original signs carried the same meaning as the derived cuneiform signs. In turn, it is logical to trust that the impressed signs perpetuated the meaning of their token prototypes.

Impressed Signs

Plain Cones, Spheres, and Flat Disks: Metrological Units of Grain(?)
Thureau Dangin in 1932 had inferred that the impressed wedges and circu- lar signs stood for metrological units used specifically for grain.[164] This is also the outcome of more recent work by A. A. Vaiman, Jöran Friberg, and Hans J. Nissen, Peter Damerov, and Robert K. Englund.[165] Friberg pro- posed that the short wedge represented a unit of grain, possibly the *ban*, the most basic Sumerian measure of cereal, which was equivalent to about 6 liters of grain. According to Friberg, a unit six times larger, the *bariga*, was represented by a circular marking.[166] It appears that the shapes of the signs for grain metrology derive from tokens in the shape of cones and spheres. The small cone apparently represented a small unit of grain in com- mon use. Moreover, the sphere is to be understood as a second, larger, basic unit of grain. Large cones and spheres represent still larger units of grain metrology. According to Friberg, the large wedge, which would corre- spond to the large cone, was equivalent to 180 *ban* of barley. The wedges shown sideways or apex to apex were fractions of a *ban*.

Furthermore, it appears to be meaningful that in the four instances when flat disks were included in envelopes, they were associated with small spheres[167] or with small and large spheres.[168] The association of spheres and flat disks in envelopes seems to correspond with the frequent association of deep and shallow circular impressed signs on tablets. I therefore propose the possibility that spheres, large spheres, and flat disks represent a se- quence of three measures of grain corresponding respectively to such later Sumerian units as 1, 10, and (?) *bariga*. These three circular signs could correspond to ATU 897, 913, and 907.

It should be assumed, however, that during prehistory, cones, spheres, and disks represented nonstandardized measures of grain. They referred probably to containers in which the goods were traditionally handled, such as a "small basket," a "large basket," or a "granary." These units might be compared to such present-day informal measures as a "cup of sugar" and a "pitcher of beer." As a result, the prehistoric units should be assumed to be entirely nonmathematical entities. Until the late fourth millennium B.C., a sphere cannot be considered as a precise multiple/fraction of a cone or disk. The measures probably did not become standardized metrological units before the late Uruk period or the early historical period, when their ratio was as follows:

CEREALS

5 — 6 — 10 — 3

BAN   BARIGA

The Punched Cones and Spheres: Units of Land Measurement(?)

The Sumerian system of land measures include such units as the *bur, eše,* and *iku* and fractions or multiples thereof represented by circular signs and wedges, some bearing a punctation or an incision.[169] The similarity in appearance of these signs with the punched cones and with the notched and punched spheres suggests that these tokens may have been used to indicate units of land. The similarity of shape between counters indicating grain and land measures may, in turn, point to a common practice in early societies of calculating land measurements in terms of the quantity of seed necessary for sowing.[170]

The tokens indicating units of land cannot be considered to have represented standardized measures during prehistory. It is only in the late fourth or early third millennium B.C. that they became increments of a specific ratio, as follows:

LAND

6 — 6 — 3 — 10

IKU   EŠE   BUR   BURU

The Cylinders and Lenticular Disks: Units for Animal Counts(?)

Jöran Friberg identified a special accounting system used to keep track of animals in Elam that was also used in Uruk.[171] These signs consisted of a long wedge, which I propose to view as the rendering of a cylinder (type 4: 1), to represent one animal. This assumption is supported by an envelope from Susa, Sb 1940, which bears three long wedges on its surface, corresponding to three cylinders held inside.[172]

According to Friberg, the sign for ten animals was a circle, which I interpret as the graphic representation of a lenticular disk (type 3: 10). This is also supported by the Susa envelope Sb 1940, which held three lenticular disks translated into three circular markings on its face.[173] If this interpre-

Grain measures: Še-system, after Jöran Friberg, *The Third Millennium Roots of Babylonian Mathematics* (Göteborg: Chalmers University of Technology and University of Göteborg, 1978–1979), p. 10.

Land measures: After Jöran Friberg, *The Third Millennium Roots of Babylonian Mathematics* (Göteborg: Chalmers University of Technology and University of Göteborg, 1978–1979), p. 46

tation is correct, the lenticular disk is a unique example of a token expressing a group. I assume that the prototype lenticular disk meant a "flock." Only in the late fourth or early third millennium can the impressed circular sign be identified as standing for a precise number: "ten animals."

Cylinders as well as lenticular disks, it seems, were used to count animals, with no specification of age and sex. Because sheep and goats were so common in Mesopotamia and Elam, it is probable that the animals in question were mostly small livestock.

Animal units: After Jöran Friberg, *The Third Millennium Roots of Babylonian Mathematics* (Göteborg: Chalmers University of Technology and University of Göteborg, 1978–1979), p. 21.

ANIMALS

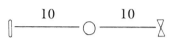

The plain tokens, which were both the most common and the most ancient counters, stood for quantities of staple foods — grain and livestock — and for measures of land. They gave rise to parallel sequences of impressed signs, the first being metrological units of cereals, the second standing for numbers of animals, and the third representing area of land. The tokens/signs of these three sequences are not often combined in a single envelope or on the same tablet. In one instance, however, lenticular disks were associated with cones in an envelope from Susa.[174] This particular account stood, perhaps, for quantities of fodder allotted to a number of animals.

In sum, the meaning of the fourth-millennium plain tokens can be extrapolated backward from the impressed signs of the fourth to the third millennia B.C. But what about the cones, spheres, disks, and cylinders extracted from the prehistoric layers of the eighth to the fifth millennia B.C.? Can one assume that they held the same significance as those of the fourth millennium? There is no way to know. The only clue they might hold is the fact that signs and symbols have a pervasive endurance which makes them withstand time in a unique fashion. This is exemplified, for example, by our symbols for numerals — 1, 2, 3, etc. — which have remained practically unchanged since their inception in 700 B.C. After all, symbols are instituted for the purpose of communication, and any deviation in their use would create miscommunication and confusion. Disjunction in symbolism, as argued by Terence Grieder, occurs only as a result of drastic social or environmental change.[175] No such upheaval is known to have occurred between the Neolithic and the Chalcolithic period in the Near East. On the contrary, that time is known as a cultural plateau characterized by a great stability.

Another vexing problem concerns whether or not cones, spheres, disks, and cylinders carried the same meaning from the Mediterranean coast to the Caspian Sea. While the question cannot be answered, several arguments offer support for the idea that they did. First, it is easier to borrow than to reinvent. Second, the cones, spheres, disks, and cylinders were among the easiest shapes to make and, according to the law of least effort, represented the most common staples: grain and animals. Now, cultivated grain and domesticated animals were common throughout the entire Near East, making it particularly easy to borrow the system wholesale. Third, the tokens were concept signs, independent of phonetics, and could be shared by people speaking different languages. Again, tokens can be compared to our numerals, which originated in India and are now used on the greatest part of the planet, standing for the same concepts for the innumerable people who express them in different languages.

Incised Signs

The tokens identified by pictographs likewise stood for units of merchandise, leading to the conclusion that during its entire existence the token system was an accounting device restricted to keeping track of goods. Some of the complex tokens were used to keep accounts of animals and quantities of grain. They differed from the plain tokens, however, in showing greater precision. Cylinders and lenticular disks represented so many head of livestock but the complex counters indicated the species ("fat-tailed sheep," type 2: 15), the sex ("ewe," type 3: 54), and the age ("lamb," type 3: 14). The quantum jump in the number of token types and subtypes which occurred in large cities about 3500 B.C. seems to reflect a need for greater accuracy.

On the other hand, most of the complex tokens found in the large centers of the fourth millennium B.C. stood for finished products, such as bread, oil, perfume, wool, and rope, and for items produced in workshops, such as metal, bracelets, types of cloth, garments, mats, pieces of furniture, tools, and a variety of stone and pottery vessels. The multiplication of token shapes in the protohistorical period, therefore, signals the addition of manufactured products to the goods accounted for in the temples.

Accordingly, plain and complex tokens varied not only in their shapes, markings, and the way they were handled and stored but also in the types of commodities they represented. The plain tokens stood for products of the countryside, the complex ones for goods manufactured in cities.

Numerals

The invention of numerals on pictographic tablets provided a new formula to express numbers of units of goods. We know from the token contents of envelopes that tokens were repeated as many times as the number of items counted. "One jar of oil" was shown by one token standing for a jar of oil; "two jars of oil" by two such tokens, "three jars of oil" by three tokens, and so on (figs. 12 and 16). This rudimentary system was replaced on pictographic tablets by numerals or signs used to express abstract numbers, such as 1, 2, 3, etc. As a result, the pictographs were *never repeated in a one-to-one correspondence* to indicate the number of units involved, as was still the case for impressed signs. Instead, the pictographs were preceded by a numeral. For example, the sign for "jar of oil" was preceded by the sign for 1, 2, 3, etc.

The sign for 1 was a short wedge, identical to the sign for a small measure of grain; 2, 3, 4, 5, etc. were indicated by two, three, four, or five wedges; the sign for 10 was a circular sign, identical to that for a larger measure of grain. In the same fashion, the sign for 60 was a large wedge; for 600, a punched large wedge; and that for 3,600, a large circular sign.[176] It appears that the impressed signs, while retaining their primary meaning as grain measures, acquired a secondary meaning as numerals. This phenomenon of bifurcation is particularly explicit on tablets where, in the same text, identical signs are used alternately to express grain measures or numerals. Tablets recording the rations allotted to workers, for example, feature the same signs to indicate the number of workers paid and the quantities of grain they received.[177] The same is true in the Proto-Elamite system of writing.[178]

Numerals created an economy of notation, since thirty-three jars of oil could be shown by six signs: three circles and three wedges. The importance of this bifurcation in the meaning of signs crucially marks a cognitive departure in the quantification of goods.

THE PLACE OF IMPRESSED TABLETS IN THE EVOLUTION OF WRITING

The impressed tablets constitute the third step in the evolution from tokens to signs. They followed the stage of tokens and markings on envelopes and, in turn, were supplanted by pictography.

The link between impressed tablets and envelopes is demonstrated by the many features they share. First, the impressed tablets adopted the same material from which envelopes were manufactured: they were modeled in clay. The tablets were also modeled in the same general shape and size as their immediate precursors. Adam Falkenstein noted that the earliest pictographic Uruk tablets were sometimes strikingly convex: perhaps they perpetuated the roundish shape of the former envelopes.[179] Of course, envelopes and tablets had a different structure. The envelopes were hollow, since their purpose was to hold and protect a number of tokens. As tokens came to be eliminated, the tablets were naturally solid.

The seal impressions covering the entire surface of most envelopes and tablets constitute another important similarity between the two types of artifacts. Not only were these sealings made by the same types of seals—namely, mostly cylinders and more rarely stamp seals—but they also showed similar patterns carved in the same style. Featured among the many motifs which occur on both types of artifacts, for example, are temple representations and various types of vessels.[180] Furthermore, occasionally at Susa[181] as well as Uruk[182] a number of tablets and envelopes bore the impression of the same seal, attesting that the two ways of keeping records were handled by the same temple services or individuals.

Most important, the signs of the impressed tablets are comparable—in form, technique, and disposition—to the signs displayed on envelopes. First, the same signs reoccur on both types of artifacts. In particular, all the markings impressed on envelopes—short and long wedges, deep and shallow circles and ovals—continue unchanged in the repertory of signs on tablets.[183] The list of signs impressed on tablets, however, is longer than that of the markings on envelopes. This may be explained by the small sampling of 19 envelopes bearing markings, compared to some 240 impressed tablets. Also, by the time tablets were in use, the scribes had already exploited further the possibilities offered by two-dimensionality, creating new signs. Thus, they manipulated the wedge, turning it sideways (sign 1d) or doubling it (sign 1e).

Second, the techniques most frequently used to impress markings on envelopes prevailed on tablets. Thus, signs were still made by pressing tokens against the clay face of the tablets, as is visibly the case on Sb 2313 (fig. 19); otherwise, it was usual to use a blunt stylus (fig. 18).

Third and finally, the signs were presented on the tablets in horizontal parallel lines, following the same hierarchical order as on the envelopes. One envelope from Susa, for example, displays a line of circular signs followed by a line of wedges, in exactly the same way signs were presented on a tablet.[184] In turn, this may reflect the hierarchical order and the parallel rows in which tokens were organized by prehistoric accountants.

The function of impressed signs and of envelope markings, however, was radically different. The discrepancy lay in the role they played vis-à-vis the clay counters. On envelopes, for the convenience of accountants, the markings merely repeated the information encoded in the tokens within. By the tablet stage, however, the signs had altogether replaced the tokens.

The format inherited from the envelopes by the impressed tablets was to enjoy a long life. Clay continued to be used to make tablets, in the same cushion shape and bearing seal impressions, until the Christian era.[185] Also, the same disposition and hierarchical ordering of signs persisted for centuries.[186] Even the function of the tablets remained mostly economic throughout the ages. The technique of writing, however, evolved from crudely impressed signs to the more legible incised pictographs and would later be done with a more functional triangular stylus.

The Interpretation PART TWO

CHAPTER FIVE

The Evolution of Symbols
in Prehistory

Individuals applied their minds to symbols rather than things and went beyond the world of concrete experience into the world of conceptual relations created within an enlarged time and space universe. The time world was extended beyond the range of remembered things and the space world beyond the range of known places. — HAROLD A. INNIS[1]

IT IS THE NATURE of archaeological research to deal with data and their interpretation. In the following three chapters I use the facts as well as the hypotheses I have presented on the token system to reflect more broadly on the significance of tokens with respect to communication, social structures, and cognitive skills.

The present chapter deals with the place of tokens among other prehistoric symbolic systems. After presenting relevant aspects of symbolism from the Paleolithic to the Neolithic period, I will analyze what the tokens owed to their antecedents, how they revolutionized the use of symbols, and how they presaged writing.

SYMBOLS AND SIGNS

Symbols are things whose special meaning allows us to conceive, express, and communicate ideas. In our society, for example, black is the symbol of death, the star-spangled banner stands for the United States of America, and the cross for Christianity.

Signs are a subcategory of symbols. Like symbols, signs are things which convey meaning, but they differ in carrying narrow, precise, and unambiguous information. Compare, for example, the color black, the symbol standing for death, with the sign "1." Black is a symbol loaded with a deep but diffuse significance, whereas 1 is a sign which stands unequivocally for the number "one." Symbols and signs are used differently: symbols help us to conceive and reflect on ideas, whereas signs are communication devices bound to action.[2]

Because the use of symbols is a characteristic of human behavior, it is by definition as old as humankind itself.[3] From the beginnings of humanity, symbols have encapsulated the knowledge, experience, and beliefs of all people. Humans, from the beginning, have also communicated by signs. Symbols and signs, therefore, are a major key to the understanding of cultures.

Symbols, however, are ephemeral and, as a rule, do not survive the societies that create them. For one thing, the meaning they carry is arbitrary. For instance, the color black, which evokes death in our culture, may just as well stand for life in another. It is a fundamental characteristic of symbols that their meaning cannot be perceived either by the senses or by logic but can only be learned from those who use them.[4] As a consequence, when a culture vanishes, the symbols left behind become enigmatic, for there is no longer anyone initiated into their significance. Thus, not only are symbolic relics from prehistoric societies extremely few, but those which are extant usually cannot be interpreted.

LOWER AND MIDDLE PALEOLITHIC SYMBOLS

Although humans were present in the Near East starting in the Lower Paleolithic period, as early as 600,000 years ago, no symbols have been preserved from these remote times. The first archaeological material attesting to the use of symbols in the Near East belongs to the epoch of Neanderthal humans, the Middle Paleolithic period, as late as 60,000 to 25,000 B.C. The data are threefold. First, pieces of ocher were recovered in the cave of Qafzeh, Israel.[5] There is, of course, no way of knowing what ocher was used for at the time, but the red pigment suggests a symbolic rather than a functional purpose, and some hypothesize it may have been used for body painting. The second set of evidence consists of funerary paraphernalia, such as flowers or antlers deposited in burial sites — for example, at Shanidar about 60,000 B.C.[6] and at Qafzeh.[7] Although we shall never know the significance that ocher, flowers, and antlers may have had for Neanderthal humans, it is generally assumed that the red pigment and the funerary deposits were symbols carrying a magico-religious connotation. Accordingly, some of the earliest evidence of the use of symbols in the Near East suggests a ritual function.

A third category of artifacts is bone fragments engraved with series of notches usually arranged in a parallel fashion, such as were recovered in the cave of Kebara.[8] These incised bones are important for the present study because they constitute the earliest known examples of manmade symbols in the Near East. Whereas at Shanidar Neanderthal humans conferred a meaning on pigments and flowers readily available in nature, the occupants of Kebara began modifying materials in order to translate ideas.

UPPER PALEOLITHIC AND MESOLITHIC SYMBOLS

The same symbolic tradition continues in the Upper Paleolithic and the Mesolithic. The use of ocher is frequently attested,[9] and notched bones are part of the assemblages at Hayonim in Israel, ca. 28,000 B.C.,[10] as well as at Jiita[11] and Ksar Akil in Lebanon, ca. 15,000–12,000 B.C. A bone awl from Ksar Akil measures about 10 cm in length and bears some 170 incisions grouped along the shaft into four separate columns (fig. 27).[12] Such arti-

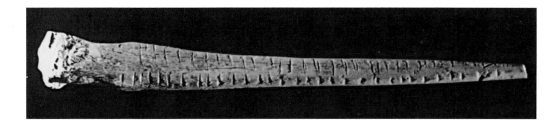

Fig. 27. Notched bone, Ksar Akil, Lebanon. Courtesy Alexander Marshack, Peabody Museum, Harvard University.

facts are still present at Hayonim,[13] at other Natufian sites of the Levant,[14] and even as far away as the Negev around 10,000 B.C.[15] At the same time, sites from the Levant to Iraq produced pebbles and various limestone and bone implements engraved with parallel lines.[16]

A new category of iconic symbols is manifested in western Asia during the course of the Upper Paleolithic. At Hayonim, ca. 28,000 B.C., these symbols take the shape of stone slabs bearing fine lines that suggest a horse.[17] The cave of Beldibi, Turkey, dated about 15,000 to 12,000 B.C., produced images of a bull and a deer, traced with a flint on the cave wall[18] and on pebbles.[19]

The function of the Paleolithic and Mesolithic incised bones and animal representations can only be hypothesized. André Leroi-Gourhan viewed the iconic representations as symbols of magico-religious significance. According to him, the animal images referred to the numinous, each species representing one manifestation of a complex cosmology.[20] Leroi-Gourhan argued that these animal figures were symbols loaded with a deep meaning, serving as instruments of thought and making it possible to grasp the abstract concepts of a cosmology. On the other hand, from the early days of archaeology, the notched bones have been interpreted as tallies, each notch representing one item of which to keep track.[21] According to a recent theory of Alexander Marshack, the artifacts were lunar calendars, each incised line recording one sighting of the moon.[22] The linear markings have been consistently viewed as referring to discrete and concrete entities. I suggest, therefore, that we consider the notches as signs promoting the accumulation of knowledge for specific ends. If these hypotheses are correct, the tallies constitute evidence that signs started being used in the Near East at least by the Middle Paleolithic period; and if the evidence reflects the facts, then the use of signs to communicate factual information followed the use of symbols in ritual.

If indeed the incised bones are tallies, the Paleolithic and Mesolithic linear markings of Kebara, Hayonim, Ksar Akil, and Jiita are of considerable interest because they represent the first attempt at storing and communicating concrete information in the Near East. This first step in "data processing" signified two remarkable contributions. First, the tallies departed from the use of ritual symbols by dealing with concrete data. They translated perceptible physical phenomena, such as the successive phases of the moon, rather than evoking intangible aspects of a cosmology. Second, the notched signs abstracted data in several ways:

1. They translated concrete information into abstract markings.
2. They removed the data from their context. For example, the sighting of the moon was abstracted from any simultaneous events such as atmospheric or social conditions.
3. They separated the knowledge from the knower, presenting data, as we are told by Walter J. Ong[23] and Marshall McLuhan, in a "cold" and static visual form, rather than in the "hot" and flexible oral medium, which involves voice modulation and body gestures.[24]

As a result, the graphic signs of Ksar Akil and Jiita not only brought about a new way of recording, handling, and communicating data, but generated an unprecedented objectivity in dealing with information.

The tallies remained, however, a rudimentary device. For one thing, the notches were unspecific and could suggest an unlimited field of interpretations. Marshack postulates that the signs stood for phases of the moon; others have hypothesized that they served to keep a tally of animal kills. But there is no way to verify their meaning. In fact, the notched bones were limited to recording quantitative information concerning things known by the tallier but remaining enigmatic to anyone else. These quantities were entered according to the basic principle of one-to-one correspondence, which consisted in matching each unit of the group to be tallied with one notch. Moreover, because tallies used a single kind of marking—namely, notches—they could handle only one type of data at a time. One bone could keep track of one item, but a second bone was necessary in order to keep track of a second set of data. Therefore, this simple method of tallies would be adequate only in communities where just a few obvious items were being recorded, as seems to have been the case in the Upper Paleolithic period.

It is certainly possible, of course, that the bone tallies were not the only devices for storing information before 10,000 B.C. It is even likely that, as in many preliterate societies, people during the Paleolithic and Mesolithic periods used pebbles, twigs, or grains for counting. If this was so, then these counters shared the same inadequacies as tallies. First of all, pebbles, like the notches along the shaft of a bone, lacked the capacity to indicate what item was being counted. Only the individual who made the markings or piled up a number of pebbles knew what things were being recorded. Second, because they were nonspecific, pebbles and twigs did not allow one to keep track of more than a single category at a time. A pile of pebbles, or one bone, could keep track of a sequence of days, but another pile and another bone would be necessary to handle quantities of, say, animals. Third and finally, it may be presumed that the loose counters were used, like tallies, in the cumbersome method of one-to-one correspondence—

each pebble or each twig standing for one unit, with no possibility of expressing abstract numbers. One day, for example, was represented by one pebble, two days by two pebbles, and so on. The loose counters facilitated data manipulation because they were easier to handle. On the other hand, the notched bones were more efficient for accumulating and preserving data, because the notches were permanent and could not be disassembled.

NEOLITHIC SYMBOLS

The first agricultural communities of the Near East carried on the age-old symbolic traditions. Early farmers placed antlers in house foundations and painted their floors with pigments.[25] They also performed burial rituals that sometimes involved red ocher.[26] At that time, too, human and animal forms were translated into clay figurines.[27] Finally, notched bones were still part of village assemblages.[28] However, the practice of agriculture generated new symbols—no doubt as a result of a new economy and a new way of life. The new symbols were different in form and content from anything used previously. These were the clay tokens modeled in distinctive shapes, each representing a precise quantity of a product.

A New Form

The primary singularity of the tokens was that they were entirely manmade. In contrast to pebbles, twigs, or grains put to a secondary use for counting, and in contrast to tallies, which communicated meaning by slightly altering a bone, tokens were artifacts created in specific shapes, such as cones, spheres, disks, cylinders, and tetrahedrons, from an amorphous clay mass for the unique purpose of communication and record keeping.

The tokens were an entirely new medium for conveying information. Here the conceptual leap was to endow each token shape, such as the cone, sphere, or disk, with a specific meaning. Consequently, unlike markings on tallies which had an infinite number of possible interpretations, each clay token was itself a distinct sign with a single, discrete, and unequivocal significance. While tallies were meaningless out of context, tokens could always be understood by anyone initiated into the system. The tokens, therefore, presaged pictography: each token stood for a single concept. Like the later Sumerian pictographs, the tokens were "concept signs."[29]

The greatest novelty of the new medium, however, was that it created a *system*. There was not just one type of token carrying a discrete meaning but an entire repertory of interrelated types of tokens, each with a corresponding discrete meaning. For example: besides the cone, which stood for a small measure of grain, the sphere represented a large measure of grain, the ovoid stood for a jar of oil, and so on. The system made it feasible to simultaneously manipulate information concerning different categories of items, resulting in a complexity of data processing never reached previously. It thus became possible to store with precision unlimited quantities of in-

formation concerning an infinite number of goods without the risk of depending on human memory. Furthermore, the system was open; that is to
say, new signs were added when necessary by creating new token shapes,
and the ever-increasing repertory constantly pushed the device to new fron-
tiers of complexity.

The token system was, in fact, the first code — the earliest system of signs
used for transmitting information. First of all, the repertory of shapes was
systematized; that is to say, all the various tokens were systematically repeated in order to carry the same meaning. A sphere, for example, always
signified a particular measure of grain. Second, it may be presumed that
tokens were used according to a rudimentary syntax. It is likely, for example, that the counters were lined up on the accountant's table in a hierarchical order, starting on the right with tokens representing the largest
units. That was how the Sumerians organized signs on a tablet, and it is
logical to assume that the procedure was inherited from former usage in
handling tokens. The fact that the tokens were systematized also had a
great impact on their expansion. The token system was transmitted as a
full-fledged code from community to community, ultimately spreading
throughout the entire Near East, with each token form preserving the same
meaning.

The token system owed little to the Paleolithic and Mesolithic periods.
The choice of material for manufacturing the counters was a novelty: clay
had been ignored by hunters and gatherers. Clay proved particularly advan-
tageous since it is found abundantly in nature and is easy to work. Its remarkable plasticity when wet made it possible for villagers to create, with
no tools and no great skill, an indefinite number of forms which became
permanent when dried in the sun or baked in an open fire or oven.

The format of movable units was probably one of the very few features
that tokens adopted from the past, perhaps having been inspired by a former usage of counting with pebbles, shells, twigs, or grains. Such a format
enhanced data manipulation, since the small tokens could be arranged and
rearranged at will into groups of any composition and size, while notches
engraved on tallies were fixed and irreversible.

Otherwise, the various token shapes have no known Paleolithic or Mesolithic antecedents. But the counters have the merit of bringing together
as a set, for the first time, each of the basic geometric shapes, such as the
sphere, cone, cylinder, tetrahedron, triangle, quadrangle, and cube (the latter surprisingly rarely).[30] It is difficult to evaluate which of these forms
were inspired by everyday life commodities and which were fully abstract.
Among the latter, the cylinders and lenticular disks, which represented, alternatively, one unit and a group of animals, are visibly arbitrary. Others,
such as the cone and ovoid, which stand respectively for a measure of
grain and a unit of oil, were probably iconic, depicting a small cup and a
pointed jar. Still other tokens, in the shape of animal heads, were naturalistic depictions.

A New Content

The token system was also unique in the kind of information it conveyed. Whereas Paleolithic iconic art probably evoked cosmological figures, and whereas Paleolithic or Mesolithic tallies may have counted time, the tokens dealt with economic data: each token stood for one precise amount of a commodity. As noted above, the cone and the sphere represented measures of grain probably equivalent to our liter and our bushel, respectively; the cylinder and lenticular disk showed numbers of animals; the tetrahedrons were units of work; and so on.

Moreover, unlike tallies, which recorded only quantitative information, the tokens also conveyed qualitative information. The type of item counted was indicated by the token shape, while the number of units involved was shown by the corresponding number of tokens. For example, one bushel of grain was represented by one sphere, two bushels of grain by two spheres, and (as shown in fig. 28) five bushels corresponded to five spheres. Therefore, like the previous tallies, the token system was based on the simple

Fig. 28. Envelope holding five spheres standing for five measures of grain(?), Susa (Sb 4828), Iran. Courtesy Musée du Louvre, Département des Antiquités Orientales.

principle of one-to-one correspondence. This made it cumbersome to deal with large quantities of data, since humans can only identify small sets by pattern recognition. There are a few instances of tokens, though, which stood for a collection of items. Among them, the lenticular disk stood for a "flock" (presumably ten sheep). The large tetrahedron may have represented a week's work or the work of a gang—compared with the small tetrahedron, expressing one man-day's work.

The tokens lacked a capacity for dissociating the numbers from the items counted: one sphere stood for "one bushel of grain," and three spheres stood for "one bushel of grain, one bushel of grain, one bushel of grain." This inability to abstract numbers also contributed to the awkwardness of the system, since each collection counted required an equal number of tokens of a special shape. Furthermore, the number of types and subtypes of tokens multiplied over time in order to satisfy the growing need for more specificity in accounting. Thus, tokens for counting sheep were supplemented by special tokens for counting rams, ewes, and lambs. This proliferation of signs was bound to lead to the system's collapse.

The Neolithic symbolic system of clay tokens superseded the Paleolithic tallies throughout the Near East because it had the following advantages:

    A. The system was simple.
     1. Clay was a common material requiring no special skills or tools to be worked.
     2. The forms of the tokens were plain and easy to duplicate.
     3. The system was based on a one-to-one correspondence, which is the simplest method for dealing with quantities.
     4. The tokens stood for units of goods. They were independent of phonetics and could be meaningful in any dialect.
    B. The code allowed new performances in data processing and communication.
     1. It was the first mnemonic device able to handle and store an unlimited quantity of data.
     2. It brought more flexibility in the manipulation of information by making it possible to add, subtract, and rectify data at will.
     3. It enhanced logic and rational decisionmaking by allowing the scrutiny of complex data.

As will be discussed in the next chapter, the code was also timely. It fulfilled new needs for counting and accounting created by agriculture. It was an intrinsic part of the "Neolithic Revolution" spreading throughout the entire region of the Near East, wherever agriculture became adopted.

A TURNING POINT IN COMMUNICATION AND DATA STORAGE

The Neolithic token system may be considered as the second step in the evolution of communication and data processing. It followed the Paleolithic and Mesolithic mnemonic devices and preceded the invention of pictographic writing in the urban period. The tokens are the link, therefore, between tallies and pictographs. They borrowed elements from such Paleolithic antecedents as the tallies or pebbles used for counting. On the other hand, the counters already presaged writing in many important ways.

The main debt of the token system to Paleolithic and Mesolithic tallies was the principle of abstracting data. Like tallies, tokens translated concrete information into abstract markings, removed the data from their context, separated the knowledge from the knower, and increased objectivity. The format of small movable counters was probably inherited from a former usage of counting with pebbles, shells, or seeds. Most important, the tokens acquired from tallies and pebbles their cumbersome way of translating quantity in one-to-one correspondence.

On the other hand, the tokens were new symbols which laid the groundwork for the invention of pictographic writing. In particular, they presaged the Sumerian writing system by the following features: [31]

1. *Semanticity:* Each token was meaningful and communicated information.
2. *Discreteness:* The information conveyed was specific. Each token shape, like each pictograph, was bestowed a unique meaning. The incised ovoid, for example, like the sign ATU 733, stood for a unit of oil.
3. *Systematization:* Each of the token shapes was systematically repeated in order to carry the same meaning. An incised ovoid, for example, always signified the same measure of oil.
4. *Codification:* The token system consisted of a multiplicity of interrelated elements. Besides the cone, which stood for a small measure of grain, the sphere represented a larger measure of grain, the ovoid meant a jar of oil, the cylinder an animal, and so on. Consequently, the token system made it feasible, for the first time, to deal simultaneously with information concerning different items.
5. *Openness:* The repertory of tokens could be expanded at will by creating further shapes representing new concepts. The tokens could also be combined to form any possible set. This made it feasible to store an unlimited quantity of information concerning an unlimited number of items.
6. *Arbitrariness:* Many of the token forms were abstract; for example, the cylinder and lenticular disk stood respectively for one and ten(?) animals. Others were arbitrary representations; for instance, the head of an animal bearing a collar symbolized the dog.
7. *Discontinuity:* Tokens of closely related shapes could refer to unrelated concepts. For example, the lenticular disk stood for ten(?) animals, whereas the flat disk referred to a large measure of grain.
8. *Independence of phonetics:* The tokens were concept signs standing for units of goods. They were independent of spoken language and

phonetics and thus could be understood by people speaking different tongues.

9. *Syntax:* The tokens were organized according to set rules. There is evidence, for example, that tokens were arranged in lines of counters of the same kind, with the largest units placed at the right.

10. *Economic content:* The tokens, like the earliest written texts, were limited to handling information concerning real goods. It is only centuries later, about 2900 B.C., that writing began to record historical events and religious texts.

The chief drawback of the token system was its format. On the one hand, three-dimensionality gave the device the advantage of being tangible and easy to manipulate. On the other hand, the volume of the tokens constituted a major shortcoming. Although they were small, the counters were also cumbersome when used in large quantities. Consequently, as is illustrated by the small number of tokens held in each envelope, the system was restricted to keeping track of small amounts of goods. The tokens were also difficult to use for permanent records, since a group of small objects can easily be separated and can hardly be kept in a particular order for any length of time. Finally, the system was inefficient because each commodity was expressed by a special token and thus required an ever-growing repertory of counters. In short, because the token system consisted of loose, three-dimensional counters, it was sufficient to record transactions dealing with small quantities of various goods but ill-suited for communicating more complex messages. Other means, such as seals, were relied upon to identify the patron/recipient in a transaction.

In turn, the pictographic tablets inherited from tokens the system of a code based on concept signs, a basic syntax, and an economic content. Writing did away with the greatest inadequacies of the token system by bringing four major innovations to data storage and communication. First, unlike a group of loose, three-dimensional tokens, pictographs held information permanently. Second, the tablets accommodated more diversified information by assigning specific parts of the field for the recording of particular data. For example, signs representing the sponsor/recipient of the transaction were systematically placed below the symbols indicating goods. In this fashion, the scribe was able to transcribe information such as "ten sheep (received from) Kurlil" even though no particular signs were available to indicate verbs and prepositions. Third, writing put an end to the repetition in one-to-one correspondence of symbols representing commodities such as "sheep" (ATU 761/ZATU 571) or "oil" (ATU 733/ZATU 393). Numerals were created. From then on, these new symbols, placed in conjunction with the signs for particular goods, indicated the quantities involved. Fourth, and finally, writing overcame the system of concept signs by becoming phonetic and, by doing so, not only reduced the repertory of symbols but opened writing to all subjects of human endeavor.

THE FIRST TRACES of visual symbols in the prehistoric Near East date to the Mousterian period, ca. 60,000–25,000 B.C. These symbols, which consisted of funerary offerings and perhaps body paintings, show that Neanderthal humans had developed rituals in order to express abstract concepts.[32] The earliest evidence of signs(?), in the form of notched tallies, also date from the Middle Paleolithic. Assuming that the archaeological data reflect the facts, those data suggest that symbolism was used both in rituals and, at the same time, for the compilation of concrete information.

From its beginnings in about 30,000 B.C., the evolution of information processing in the prehistoric Near East proceeded in three major phases, each dealing with data of increasing specificity. First, during the Middle and late Upper Paleolithic, ca. 30,000–12,000 B.C., tallies referred to one unit of an unspecified item. Second, in the early Neolithic, ca. 8000 B.C., the tokens indicated a precise unit of a particular good. With the invention of writing, which took place in the urban period, ca. 3100 B.C., it was possible to record and communicate the name of the sponsor/recipient of the merchandise, formerly indicated by seals.

The Neolithic tokens constitute a second step, and a major turning point, in information processing. They inherited from Paleolithic devices the method of abstracting data. The system of tokens can be credited as the first use of signs to manipulate concrete commodities of daily life, whereas Paleolithic symbols dealt with ritual and whereas tallies (perhaps) recorded time. The simple but brilliant invention of clay symbols which represented basic concepts provided the first means of supplementing language. It opened new avenues of tremendous importance for communication, providing the immediate background for the invention of writing.

Tokens: The Socioeconomic Implications

As a cultural system becomes institutionalized and achieves greater growth, there inevitably results greater abstraction. — RAYMOND L. WILDER [1]

IN THE PRESENT CHAPTER, I will show how society influenced each phase of the development of prehistoric reckoning technology. Tallies, plain tokens, and complex tokens were different because each fulfilled the needs of a distinct economy and social organization. Writing, on the other hand, was the result of other stimuli.

RECKONING TECHNOLOGY AND ECONOMY

Economic life influenced prehistoric reckoning technologies by dictating what was being counted. Tallies, plain tokens, and complex tokens kept track of vastly different items: the former recorded time, whereas the latter two computed agricultural products and manufactured goods.

Hunting and Gathering

Contrary to a common misconception, the exchange of goods seems to play no role in the development of reckoning technology, presumably because during the Paleolithic period, foodstuffs and raw materials were traded on a reciprocal basis, which did not call for any accounting or record keeping.[2] There is no visible link between either tallies or tokens and the long-distance traffic in obsidian. It is well documented that this volcanic glass was already exchanged in the Mesolithic period, prior to the invention of clay counters. As with other goods, this trade did not require accounting, for obsidian too was bartered or presented as a ceremonial gift.[3] The transactions were carried out face to face and, like local trade, did not need recording.[4]

According to Alexander Marshack, the first item counted was time. Each notch engraved on a bone represented one sighting of the moon.[5] The theory that tallies were calendars is plausible because lunar notations would make it possible for dispersed communities to gather at intervals to reaffirm their ties and celebrate rituals.

Farming

What was it that made accounting necessary in 8000 B.C.? For an entirely new token system was created at that time to keep track of goods. The earliest clay counters consisted mostly of plain spheres, cones, disks, and cylinders. Since these tokens seem to stand for quantities of cereal and units of animal count, we may conclude that grain and flocks played a predominant role in the first accounting.

Mureybet, in Syria, presents convincing evidence that the invention of tokens was directly related to the cultivation of cereals. The site, occupied between 8500 and 7000 B.C., was first settled (levels I and II) by a hunting and gathering community which did not use clay counters. Tokens appeared in level III, about 8000 B.C., coinciding with the first signs of agriculture.[6] The synchronic occurrence of tokens and plant domestication in Mureybet III was not coincidental; rather, it demonstrates that agriculture brought about a need for accounting. In fact, in each of the five sites which yielded the earliest tokens, the invention of clay counters was consistently related to evidence that grain was harvested or hoarded. Sickle blades were part of the tool kit at Tepe Asiab and Ganj Dareh.[7] Silos were an important feature at Mureybet III, Cheikh Hassan, and Tell Aswad.[8]

Local and long-distance trade continued to have little impact on reckoning in the Neolithic. This is shown by the striking discrepancy between the distribution of sites yielding obsidian and those holding tokens. Ganj Dareh, for example, had tokens but no obsidian, while Çatal Hüyük had plenty of obsidian but no tokens.[9]

Industry

Industry gave a major boost to the token system, as shown by the multiplication of new types and subtypes of fourth-millennium tokens standing for manufactured goods. The complex tokens featured finished products typical of urban workshops, such as textiles, garments, vessels, and tools; processed foods, such as oil, bread, cakes, and trussed ducks; and luxury goods, such as perfume, metal, and jewelry.

The development of complex tokens was not, however, related to trade. Quite to the contrary, the deep sounding of Uruk shows no correspondence between the volume of imported raw materials, such as alabaster, flint, obsidian, and copper, and the frequency of tokens.[10] Although the temple was probably involved in securing these substances from distant markets, that involvement is not reflected in the records.

Nor is there the slightest indication that any of the tokens included in envelopes, or any of the signs on impressed tablets, stood for imported luxury goods. The evidence consists mostly of plain tokens and impressed signs representing, presumably, local agricultural staples such as grain and animals. The few complex tokens (e.g., parabolas) included in the Uruk envelopes stood seemingly for such typical Sumerian products as garments.

Moreover, the quantities handled are typically small: the tokens included in envelopes represent the equivalent of about five bushels of grain, or five *sila* of oil, which could hardly sustain any sizable long-distance trade.

The impressed and pictographic tablets continued to deal with the same kinds of goods as the token system, and in the same quantities, showing that writing was not indebted to any visible change in the economy. The Uruk tablets, like the envelopes filled with counters and the strings of tokens at Habuba Kabira, recorded small amounts of basic products such as grain, animals, oil, garments, and textiles.[11]

In sum, developments in farming and industry played a major role in the development of the token system. Cultivation of cereals was directly related to the invention of plain tokens, and the complex counters are linked to the beginning of industry. Trade, however, played no visible role in the creation of reckoning technology.

RECKONING TECHNOLOGY AND SOCIAL ORGANIZATION

Social organization determined the function of counting. After changes in the economy, it was the second most significant factor in the development of prehistoric reckoning technology.

There are two main functions of counting: computing and accounting. *Computing* consists of making calculations. *Accounting,* on the other hand, entails keeping track of entries and withdrawals of commodities. It is my contention that, computing (of time) took place within egalitarian societies, but that the origin of accounting must be assigned to ranked societies and the state. In other words, it was not simply hoarding grain or producing manufactured goods that brought about accounting: social structures played a significant role.

Egalitarian Societies

There is no archaeological evidence for accounting during the Paleolithic period. Nor is that fact surprising: hunters and gatherers subsist essentially from daily catches and do not accumulate much in the way of goods.[12] The hunter-gatherer economy, therefore, had no need for accounting, and neither did their social organization. It is assumed that Paleolithic societies were egalitarian and that, as in modern hunting-and-gathering societies, each individual received a specific share of the common resources according to his status (again, requiring no accounting or record keeping).[13] Tallies for computing time, it would appear, met all the counting needs of Paleolithic groups prior to the rise of a formal social organization.

Rank Societies

Tokens constitute the first evidence for accounting. They were not a corollary of mere farming but, rather, of the social structures which derived from agriculture. I borrow the term *rank society,* coined by Morton Fried, to express the organizational changes which became necessary for maintaining stability in village farming communities.[14] The most important aspect of these social changes with respect to the present study is the creation of an elite overseeing a redistributive economy.[15] It is assumed that ranked societies had redistribution as a major factor in their economy, with the headman acting as central collector and redistributor.[16] The fact that tokens were directly implemented in these events is suggested by three sets of data: (1) the context of the first counters at Mureybet; (2) the tokens laid in burials; and (3) the textual and art evidence of the late fourth and third millennia B.C.

The First Tokens at Mureybet

At Mureybet the first tokens coincided with farming and with a considerable demographic growth. Mureybet III expanded from a small compound of .5 hectare to a village of 2 or 3 hectares.[17] It is difficult to evaluate the size of the population, but it is thought that the community would have exceeded three hundred individuals, the maximum number considered manageable by an egalitarian system. The first token assemblage of Mureybet III coincided, then, with a new social organization.[18]

Tokens as Funerary Offerings

Because of the rarity of funerary tokens, together with their association with rich burial deposits and with artifacts symbolizing power, we know that the counters belonged not to the masses but to a privileged elite. Tomb 107 at Tepe Gawra, the only interment associated with a shrine, was surely the tomb of an important individual.[19] The fact that his funerary offerings consisted of nothing more than six spheres implies that the counters were a status symbol. The use of counters as status symbols in prehistory is not surprising. Indeed, it is to be expected that numeracy in prehistory played the same role as literacy in historical times. Consequently, the individuals who practiced the art of counting in prehistory enjoyed the same prestige as the scribes in later times.

Furthermore, the isolated deposits of tokens in the children's graves of Tell es-Sawwan and Tepe Gawra support the common view that the youths were the progeny of members of the elite.[20] In this case, tokens perhaps signified that the children were not only destined to power but were to be trained in the art of counting. The high status of preliterate administrators is not unique to the ancient Near East but is instead a common phenomenon. In fact, the use of counting devices as status symbols in funerary settings is a tradition known in distant societies. It was customary among the Incas of Peru, for example, to bury high officials with their quipus.[21]

Textual Evidence

The token system implemented the redistributive economy. The economic tablets of the fourth and third millennia serve to illustrate how prehistoric counters played the same role as writing during the historical period.

Third Millennium B.C. In the Early Dynastic period, writing dealt with temple and palace administration. The tablets of Tello recorded with scrupulous detail the movement of goods in and out of the palace and the temples.[22] Entries consisted of yields from the estates and offerings from worshipers. Disbursements were rations of barley, beer, and other commodities allotted to members of the royal family and to temple dependents, as well as expenditures for sacrifice, fodder for the flocks, and so on. The most obvious function of writing, therefore, was keeping account of the resources generated by the palace and the temple and recording their redistribution.

Another, more important function of writing was one of control. The tablets were official receipts of commodities delivered by individuals or guilds. They registered the following: (1) the items received and their quantity; (2) the name of the donor; (3) the date of the delivery, that is to say, a certain festival celebrated at the temple in honor of a divinity; and (4) the administrator who checked the commodities. It now seems well established that the so-called gifts for the gods, listed on the tablets, were in fact mandatory. High officials, for example, were required to present a lamb or a kid at the monthly festival celebrated at the temple, whereas fishermen had to produce a specific quantity of fish.[23] The written receipts made it possible for the leadership to regulate the amount of goods to be contributed by the community and to enforce their delivery. Writing, therefore, bestowed on the ruler effective control over the input of assets. By making the administration accountable for the goods received, the written receipts also conveyed mastery over the redistribution of these commodities. In other words, writing endowed the third-millennium kings with full control over communal resources. Writing was the backbone of the economy of redistribution — an economy that brought prosperity to Sumer.

Jemdet Nasr Period Like those of the third millennium, the economic texts of Uruk III, or the Jemdet Nasr period (dated 3000–2900 B.C.), served to control the input and output of communal goods. At Uruk, the tablets belonged to the temple of the goddess Inanna. Like the tablets of Tello, they featured (1) small quantities of goods, (2) the name of an individual, probably the donor, (3) the symbol of a god, presumably at whose festival the offering was made, and (4) an administrative service identified by a seal.

Uruk Period In turn, it is clear that the fourth-millennium tokens, held by strings or enclosed in envelopes, assumed the same function of control in the redistributive economy as the tablets. Tokens and pictographic tablets belonged to the same temple areas and dealt with identical goods in similar quantities. At Uruk, tablets, envelopes, and tokens belonged to the same Eanna precinct. The symbols used in both media refer to the same commodities — mostly grain, animals, textiles, and garments. The small number of tokens enclosed in each envelope corresponds with the small quantities of goods recorded on the third-millennium tablets.

The textual evidence of the protoliterate period demonstrates that, before kingship, the main components of the Near Eastern redistributive system already consisted of (1) a religious ideology, (2) a leadership acting as the central collector and redistributor, (3) laborers generating a surplus, and (4) a reckoning technology to administer/control the goods. Like the third-millennium cuneiform tablets, the pictographic records were the key to a privileged access to community properties and the key to power.

The Art Evidence

The delivery of offerings was a leitmotiv of Sumerian art in the third millennium B.C., as it was of the cuneiform tablets. Relief carvings show the king and his queen(?) banqueting while commoners deliver offerings, including animals on the hoof and jars of goods (fig. 29). The scene probably depicts the pomp of monthly festivals organized at the temple, when offerings were delivered in honor of deities of the Sumerian pantheon. The motif, in other words, illustrates how temple, king, and commoners interacted in the economy of redistribution.[24]

The famous vase of Uruk III leaves no doubt that the economy of redistribution was already ritualized by the end of the fourth millennium B.C. It features a procession of nude worshipers who, carrying jars and baskets, are following the priest-king, or En; in festive attire, wearing a long kilt, the En is proceeding toward the gate of the Inanna temple, where accumulated goods are shown (fig. 30).

The seals of the Uruk period further illustrate that an economy of redistribution was already in place by 3500 B.C. Time and time again, they depict lines of worshipers bringing food and luxury goods to the temple,[25] whereas the priest-king contributes an animal. These images demonstrate that the temple economy of redistribution was already perfected.

Fig. 29. Perforated plaque, Khafaje (A.12417), Iraq. After Pierre Amiet, *La Glyptique méso-potamienne archaïque* (Paris: Editions du CNRS, 1980), pl 93: 1222.

Fig. 30. Sculpture on a stone vase, Uruk, Iraq. After André Parrot, *Sumer* (Paris: Librairie Gallimard, 1960), fig. 89.

In sum, the art and cuneiform texts of the better-known third millennium B.C. offer an insight into the meaning and function of the more enigmatic protoliterate texts and the tokens that preceded them. The depictions of banquets and gift presentations in various art forms suggest that, during the period from 3500 to 2500 B.C., Sumer had a redistribution economy involving three main components: (1) a temple which conferred meaning and pomp on the act of giving; (2) an elite who administered the communal property; and (3) commoners who produced surplus goods and surrendered them to the temple. This redistributive economy relied upon a system of record keeping and, indeed, could not have succeeded without it. This function was fulfilled in the third millennium B.C. by cuneiform writing and, going further back in time, by pictographic writing and tokens.

The State

Plain tokens were linked to the rise of rank society, but it was the advent of the state which was responsible for the phenomenon of complex tokens.

Complex counters belong to the Mesopotamian temple institution, where they coincided with such socioeconomic changes as monumental architecture, the monopoly of force, and bureaucracy which point to new strategies in pooling communal resources.

Complex Tokens and The Rise of the South Mesopotamian Temple

The chronology of the complex tokens as established by the deep sounding of Eanna shows that complex counters came and went with the rise and fall of the Uruk temple. The first complex tokens coincided with the establishment of the sanctuary and with the decoration of public architecture with cone mosaics; the token system was at its peak during the precinct's era of splendor; and, finally, the disappearance of the counters coincided with the destruction of Eanna in level IVa. The direct relationship of this new accounting device — complex tokens — with the development of the Mesopotamian temple is significant because it implies that the changes in the token system played a role in the rise of the state.

Changes in Redistribution: Taxation

The emergence of the temple brought a major transformation to the economy of redistribution by establishing taxation — i.e., the obligation for all individuals or guilds to deliver a fixed amount of goods in kind, under penalty of sanctions. The complex tokens played a part in the collection of taxes and tribute that is typical of a state economy.

Monumental Architecture Monumental architecture required a quantum jump in the amount of resources available to the community, implying a system of taxation. The Uruk Stone Cone Temple in levels VI–V of Eanna, covered with colorful stone mosaics, or the Limestone Temple in level V meant large expenditures for materials. It is not surprising, therefore, that the earliest monumental structures corresponded with new ways of pooling surpluses, as well as with new ways of administering those surpluses, including a more precise accounting method. The construction of public buildings also required a large work force, suggesting new ways of controlling labor, such as the corvée (i.e., labor exacted from individuals at little or no pay or instead of taxes).

Changes in Leadership: The Monopoly of Force The levying of taxes also presupposes a coercive system to enforce their collection. The South Mesopotamian temple was the catalyst that produced a new type of leader, one who had the power of sanctions. This important development in political authority may be illustrated by sealings picturing nude men, hands tied at the back, being clubbed in the En's presence (fig. 31).[26] This motif has often been viewed as representing prisoners of war, but the fact that the individuals are not shown with the unusual hairdos denoting foreigners in Sumerian art suggests that we may just as well interpret this scene as depicting the sanctions needed to enforce the delivery of dues to the temple.

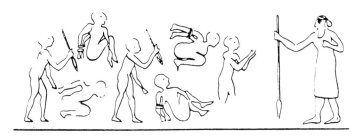

Fig. 31. Corporal
punishment, cylinder
seal impression, Uruk,
Iraq. After Pierre Amiet,
*La Glyptique méso-
potamienne archaïque*
(Paris: Editions du
CNRS, 1980), pl. 47:
660–661.

The Development of Bureaucracy   Tax collection increased the need for as-
sembling, manipulating, and storing more data with greater accuracy.
This explains the appearance of new methods for controlling goods: complex tokens, envelopes, bullae, cylinder seals, and a system of weights and
measures.

Taxation put new demands on the fourth-millennium bureaucracy
which were fulfilled by the complex tokens. The new system, utilizing a
greater variety of counters, made it possible to keep a more accurate account of the dues delivered to the temple. Complex tokens indicated with
greater specificity the species, age, and gender of animals. For example, they
differentiated between rams, ewes, or lambs, whereas the plain cylinders
simply acknowledged numbers of unspecified domesticates. Complex tokens recorded quantities of wheat or barley, whereas the plain cones and
spheres simply stood for quantities of grain. The multiplication of counter
shapes and markings also denotes a quantum jump in the number of items
accounted for. The additional shapes show that the levied commodities included processed foods (bread, oil, or trussed ducks), manufactured products (wool, cloth, garments, mats, rope, pieces of furniture, and tools), and
precious materials (perfume and metal). The novelty, obviously, was not
the existence of such items as bread, oil, cloth, pots, axes, and perfume;
these had been around for a long time. What was new was that manufactured and finished products were being *accounted for*, which had not been
true previously.

Even more important, the levy of taxes made it necessary to keep track
of what had *not* been delivered, what was still owed to the temple. The

accounting for unpaid taxes, in turn, increased the need for archives, perhaps explaining the invention of envelopes and bullae. Accordingly, the preserved accounts may have represented payments to be completed at a future date — for example, after the next harvest. This would account for the many sealings featured on each envelope, since differing payments would involve the authorization of several echelons in the administrative hierarchy. As Enrica Fiandra suggests, the two, three, and four seals applied on envelopes and solid bullae could correspond to signatures at several hierarchical levels, such as accountants, controllers, supervisors, or superintendents.[27]

The changes in the token system did not occur in isolation but coincided with a major transformation in the practice of sealing goods. Cylinder seals replaced the former stamp seals. The continuous imprint produced by cylinder seals was more efficient for authenticating goods and records. Moreover, the depiction of entire scenes on the sealings brought new possibilities of communicating information.

Finally, the creation of weights and measures in the Uruk period demonstrated a greater concern for precision in handling goods.[28] Thomas W. Beale has made the case that the beveled-rim bowls recovered by the thousands in the major fourth-millennium sites served as measuring devices.[29] There can be no doubt that all these administrative innovations were responses to the profound socioeconomic changes that surrounded the birth of the state — in particular, to the need for enforcement of deliveries of goods owed to the temple.

The Levy of Tribute   Complex counters occurred not only in Mesopotamia but also in Elam and Syria. In all three regions, however, the phenomenon was restricted to sites such as Susa and Habuba Kabira, which shared the same monumental architecture decorated with cone mosaics,[30] cylinder seals featuring the En, beveled-rim bowls, envelopes, and bullae. This distinctive bureaucratic assemblage, which is the hallmark of Uruk, indicates a Mesopotamian presence in neighboring countries and probably identifies places paying tribute to the South Mesopotamian temple. The splendors of Eanna V and VI may be explained by the influx of tribute from neighboring regions, and it could even be postulated that complex tokens, envelopes, and bullae were instrumental in that process.

IN THIS CHAPTER I have discussed how the function of the tallies and tokens reflected the economy and the political system of the cultures that used them. Whereas simple reckoning was sufficient in hunting and gathering societies, the economy of redistribution typical of the ancient Near East made accounting necessary. The plain counters used to pool communal resources in pre-urban economies were no longer adequate for the early state bureaucracy. Complex tokens were developed to handle with greater efficiency and precision the larger volume of goods generated by taxation and the levy of tribute.

Counting and the Emergence of Writing

Mathematics is, of course, a part of culture. Every people inherits from its predecessors or contemporary neighbors, along with ways of cooking, marrying, worshiping, etc., ways of counting, calculating, and whatever else mathematics does. . . . Whether a people counts by fives, tens, twelves or twenties; whether it has no words for cardinal numbers beyond 5, or possesses the most modern and highly developed mathematical conceptions, their mathematical behavior is determined by the mathematical culture which possesses them. — LESLIE A. WHITE[1]

IN THIS CHAPTER I shall argue that each reckoning device was determined by a particular mode of counting. Tallies, tokens, and writing reflected three major phases in the development of counting: (1) one-to-one correspondence, (2) concrete counting, and (3) abstract counting. Finally, I postulate that writing is the outcome of abstract counting.

Before I start the discussion, some basic terms must be defined. Our way of counting is *abstract counting*. Our numbers 1, 2, 3, for example, express the concepts of oneness, twoness, and threeness as abstract entities divorced from any particular concrete entities. As a result, our 1, 2, and 3 are universally applicable. *Numerals* are written signs such as 1, 2, and 3. *Number words* are the way people express these concepts in a particular language — for example, in English, "one," "two," "three"; or, in French, "un," "deux," "trois." *Concrete numbers* refer to concepts, like "twin," that fuse together a notion of number with that of the item counted.

THE VARIOUS MODES OF COUNTING

Raymond Wilder is among the historians of mathematics who consider our way of counting to be the result of a long evolution.[2] Following Bertrand Russell's famous statement that "it . . . required many ages to discover that a brace of pheasants and a couple of days were both instances of the number 2,"[3] Wilder and others postulate that abstract counting was preceded by more archaic modes of counting.[4]

One, Two, Many

Anthropology and linguistics suggest that people are born with only a vague sense of numbers, perhaps limited to differentiating groups of up to three objects. This idea is supported by the fact that, until the last century, societies in various parts of the world had a vocabulary limited to three number words equivalent to "one," "two," and "many."[5] For example, the

Weddas of Sri Lanka are known to have only a few number idioms, corresponding to "a single," "a pair," "one more," and "many."[6]

One-to-One Correspondence

The Weddas "counted" as much as was necessary to cope with the necessities of their everyday life: they counted in one-to-one correspondence. When a Wedda wished to count coconuts, he collected a heap of sticks. To each coconut he assigned a stick: one nut = one stick. For each stick added, he counted "and one more" until all the coconuts were tallied. Then he merely pointed to his pile of sticks and said, "That many." The example of the Weddas is enlightening because it exemplifies a basic way of counting which does not require a number system.

Concrete Counting

Counting beyond three was achieved at a different pace and in different ways in various societies, giving rise to multiple systems of counting. Among these systems, body counting — which consists in pointing to fingers, wrist, shoulder, head, nose, etc. to express particular numbers — is still practiced in some cultures.[7] Concrete counting is another widespread archaic counting system. Here, "one," "two," "three," etc. are tied to the objects counted, which means that different things are counted with different number words. Franz Boas reported on cultures which had different sets of numbers to count men, canoes, long objects, flat objects, round objects or time, measures, and other items.[8] Igor Diakonoff describes other societies which had no fewer than twenty-four classes of numbers.[9] The complexity of concrete counting, moreover, could be compounded by the fact that each numeration can have a different base. Thus, Jack Goody relates that when he asked his LoDagaa informant (Northern Ghana) to count for him, the answer was "Count what?" because, in that culture, counting cows was different from counting shells.[10]

Abstract Counting

The cumbersome handling of data by means of one-to-one correspondence, body counting, or concrete counting highlights the advantages of our own system of computing. In our society, 1, 2, 3, etc. express numbers independently from the item counted. We count men, canoes, trees, or anything else under the sun, even imaginary things, with the same numbers. Whereas concrete counting probably did not allow counting beyond a score of objects, there is no limit to abstract counting. We can count all the stars of the universe and all the grains of sand on the beach, and we can even add the total sand grains to the total stars. This was altogether impossible with concrete counting, which was confined to handling data of only one kind at a time: triplets could not be added to trios.

THE SUMERIAN PHILOLOGICAL EVIDENCE

COUNTING
AND THE
EMERGENCE
OF WRITING

113

How does all this apply to tallies and tokens? What do we know about counting in the ancient Near East? Starting with the reasonably well understood texts of the third millennium B.C., at least, there is no doubt that the Sumerians counted abstractly, just as we do.

Ternary Numeration Systems

It has been suggested, however, that the Sumerian language contains the vestiges of archaic counting systems used in former times. Several features in the Sumerian counting system suggest that, as in other societies, "three," may well have been a major hurdle to overcome in ancient Mesopotamia.[11] For example, the fact that in the main numeration, /eš/ = "three" is the same as /eš/ the plural morpheme[12] has been interpreted as reflecting a bygone, distant tradition of counting to a maximum of "three," which also meant "many."

Furthermore, several Sumerian numerations based on a three-count system[13] suggest that abstract counting in the Near East may have been preceded by an archaic concrete counting system which used different numerations to count different items. These numerations are as follows:[14]

1.	merga	=	"one"
2.	taka	=	"two" (not attested)
3.	peš	=	"three"
4.	pešbala	=	"three-passed"
5.	pešbalage	=	"three-passed-one"
6.	pešbalagege	=	"three-passed-one-one"
7.	pešpešge	=	"three-three-one"[15]

1.	ge	=	"one"
2.	dah	=	"two"
3.	PEŠ	=	"three"
4.	PEŠ-ge	=	"three + one"
5.	PEŠ-bala-gi_4	=	"three-passed-one"
6.	PEŠ-bala-gi_4-gi_4	=	"three-passed-one-one"
7.	PEŠ-PEŠ-gi_4	=	"three-three-one"

1.	be	=	"one"
2.	be-be	=	"one-one"
3.	PEŠ	=	"three"
4.	PEŠ-be	=	"three-one"
5.	PEŠ-be-be	=	"three-one-one"
6.	PEŠ-PEŠ	=	"three-three"
7.	PEŠ-PEŠ-be	=	"three-three-one"
12.	PEŠ-PEŠ-PEŠ-PEŠ	=	"three-three-three-three"

Multiplicity of Number Words

Marvin Powell has noted the multiplicity of expressions for rendering "one," "two," and "three." He remarks that lexical texts list seven Sumerian equivalents to the Akkadian *išten* = one. These numbers are as follows, "aš," "santak₃," "diš,"[16] "deli," "be," "giš" and "ge."[17] There are also several forms for "2" ("min" and "man," "taka," "dah," and "be-be") and two forms for "3" ("eš," and "peš"). Powell suggests that the different number words attested in Sumerian texts may reflect several dialects.[18]

On the other hand, Diakonoff views the multiplicity of number words in Sumerian as possible evidence for a former tradition of concrete counting. He compares the different forms of number words with concrete numerations, and proposes that concrete counting may have preceded abstract counting in Mesopotamia. Diakonoff's argument is supported by the fact that, in Sumer, the earlier the texts are, the more complex are the numerical systems they exhibit.[19] As A. A. Vaiman noted, the fourth-millennium Uruk tablets used different numeral sequences for recording area, weight, volume, and capacity measures — and even for quantities of wheat, barley, domesticated animals, slaves, and time.[20] Following his lead, Hans J. Nissen, Peter Damerow, and Robert K. Englund have identified in the archaic texts of Uruk thirteen different systems of number signs, some using ten as a base, others using six.[21] The fact that quantities of different commodities were recorded with different signs can hardly be interpreted as denoting the pronunciations of various dialects. Furthermore, Vaiman, and after him Jöran Friberg, demonstrated that the multiplicity of signs for recording different quantities of goods was not a phenomenon unique to Sumer but was also attested in Proto-Elamite.[22] This too suggests that in the Near East, as in other parts of the world, concrete counting preceded the invention of abstract counting.

THE NEAR EASTERN ARCHAEOLOGICAL DATA

The unique sequence of reckoning devices produced by Near Eastern archaeological sites of 15,000 to 3000 B.C. seems to confirm that one-to-one correspondence and concrete counting preceded the use of abstract counting in Southwest Asia.

The Paleolithic Tallies

Paleolithic notched bones, used in the Near East about 15,000 – 10,000 B.C., may well illustrate the simplest form of counting: one-to-one correspondence. Each notch probably tallied one unit of a collection. According to Alexander Marshack's hypothesis, each notch may have translated one sighting of the moon.[23] It is likely (keep in mind the ethnographic and linguistic data presented above) that the Stone Age tallies did not involve abstract counting or even a system of numbers but, rather, consisted of the repeated addition of one unit. Like most preliterate societies, the Paleolithic cultures of the Near East seem to have counted in one-to-one correspondence.

Tokens

Tokens were still used in one-to-one correspondence. However, the two-fold innovation they brought—cardinality and object specificity—seems indicative of a second stage of counting.

Cardinality

The most significant change was cardinality—the ability to assign arbitrary tags, such as number words, to each item of a collection, with the final number word of the series representing the number of the set. For example, it is likely that the *seven* incised ovoids held in an Uruk envelope stood for "*seven* jars of oil" (not "and one more," or "many," as would have been the case in the previous stage).

Tokens such as tetrahedrons, which occurred in two distinct subtypes ("small" and "large," type 5: 1 and 2), may also prove that accounting with tokens implied a grasp of the notion of sets. Tetrahedrons may have represented two different units of labor, respectively indicating "one day" and "one week's work," or they may have referred to numbers of workmen, such as "one man" and "a gang."[24] The lenticular disk (type 3: 3) is another such example. If it stood for "ten animals," the disk would prove that during the Neolithic, counting animals no longer entailed adding "and one more" but, rather, that each token served as a tag to represent a number. Cardinality resulted, therefore, in a considerable economy of notation since thirty animals could be indicated by three tokens instead of by thirty.

One-to-One Correspondence

That the token system retained the archaic principle of one-to-one correspondence during the entire duration of the system is demonstrated by the groups of counters held in envelopes. Examples of envelopes from Uruk, Susa, and Habuba Kabira reveal tokens of a single subtype repeated as many times as the number units represented. One envelope, for instance, contained seven ovoids, seemingly standing for seven jars of oil (fig. 12); another held five spheres, representing five measures of grain (fig. 28).

The content of these envelopes demonstrates unambiguously that the fourth-millennium accountants indicated quantities (how many) in a way radically different from ours. They did not indicate, as we do, "5" by a numeral. Instead, "5 jars of oil" were translated by five tokens, each standing for "1 jar of oil," as illustrated here:

This set of tokens meant literally "jar of oil, jar of oil, jar of oil, jar of oil, jar of oil." The token system had no symbols for abstract numbers.

Other envelopes clearly illustrate that tokens standing for sets were also used in one-to-one correspondence. Sb 1940, for example (fig. 15), yields an account of 33 animals, shown by 3 disks and 3 cylinders as follows:

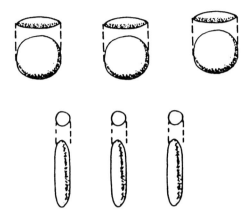

or, literally, 10 animals + 10 animals + 10 animals + 1 animal + 1 animal + 1 animal.

Object Specificity

One peculiarity of the token system was that it required a particular type of counter to deal with each type of commodity. Ovoids were used to count jars of oil, and spheres to count measures of grain; likewise, jars of oil could only be counted with ovoids, and measures of grain could only be counted with spheres. The fact that tokens varied with each commodity counted suggests that the tokens were designed to manipulate data within a system of concrete counting. Like concrete numerations, the tokens fused together the concept of number and the concept of the item counted; thus, an ovoid stood for both "1" and "jar of oil," without any possibility of abstracting the two concepts.

The Absence of Tokens Expressing Abstract Numbers

Although the notion of sets seems to have been acquired, counting with tokens still differed fundamentally from abstract counting. There were no counters standing for abstract numbers such as 1, 2, 3, etc. that could be applied to a wide range of goods.

The token system, which coincided with agriculture, the storage of goods, and an economy of redistribution, suggests that such innovations brought pressure for counting beyond three. Moreover, the multiplicity of counters indicates that the first farmers had mastered the notion of sets, or cardinality, but still counted concretely. In other words, they had no conception of numbers that existed independently of measures of grain and animals and that could be applied to either commodity without reference to the other. The token system, then, supports the linguistic data that concrete counting preceded abstract counting in the prehistoric Near East.

Concrete counting provides the key to understanding the greatest peculiarity of the token system: namely, the multiplicity of counters. Previous attempts at assigning numerical values to particular tokens fail to jibe with the evidence. Alain Le Brun and François Vallat, who assumed that the token system relied upon our own system of abstract counting, proposed the following translations: cylinder 1; sphere 10; disk 100; cone 60, 600, or 1,000; punched cone 300; and punched sphere 36,000.[25] Their interpretation, however, leaves the remaining four hundred or so subtypes of complex counters without explanation.

Following Le Brun and Vallat, Stephen J. Lieberman proposed that the plain tokens were counters representing numbers, whereas the complex ones were "small clay objects of unknown use."[26] As discussed in Chapter 1 above, the argument that plain and complex tokens did not belong to the same reckoning device does not correspond to the evidence. Both are found together at the same sites, in the same levels, and in the same hoards. Envelopes at Uruk and Habuba Kabira held complex tokens (incised ovoids) (figs. 12 and 16). Why would complex tokens be enclosed in envelopes if they were not used as counters?

Pierre Amiet's view that lines and dots marked on tokens were numerical notations must also be dismissed.[27] There is no evidence that, for instance, the ovoid bearing six punctations meant "six jars of oil" (type 6: 22). For the above-noted envelopes of Uruk and Habuba Kabira clearly demonstrate that the number of jars of oil was shown by repeating the ovoids in one-to-one correspondence, not by means of markings. Impressed signs further demonstrate the point. Consider, for instance, the tablet from Susa which shows four impressions of a triangular token with one incised line (type 8: 11; fig. 22) If Amiet's interpretation were correct, the notation would consist of a triangle with four lines. The fact that the triangle (but not the marking) was repeated four times indicates that markings referred to the quality of a commodity, not to the number.

Writing

Impressed Markings on Envelopes and Tablets
When tokens were replaced by their images impressed on the surface of an envelope or a tablet, the resulting impressed markings were identical semantically to tokens: each ideogram fused together the concepts of nature/quantity (i.e., measure of oil) and the number 1. For example, each of the incised ovoids impressed on a Habuba Kabira envelope (fig. 16) or the incised triangles shown on a tablet from Susa (fig. 22) indicated respectively "1 measure of oil" and "1 unit of ?" in one-to-one correspondence. Friberg is wrong in assuming that the impressed tablets are governed by the same counting system as the one used in the classical Sumerian period, when units were represented in one-to-one correspondence until they could be replaced by the next larger unit. Whereas in the third millennium B.C. five large measures of grain were translated by five circular markings but six large measures of grain were translated by one large wedge, this was not so

on the impressed tablets. This is clearly demonstrated by several tablets bearing twenty-two, ten, or nine circular markings to represent twenty-two, ten, or nine large units of grain (fig. 24) in one-to-one correspondence.[28] The impressed envelopes and tablets illustrate, therefore, that the Uruk IV notations still did not express abstract numbers.

The First Numerals

The accountants of Uruk IVa, about 3100 B.C, invented the first numerals — signs encoding the concept of oneness, twoness, threeness, etc. abstracted from any particular entity. This was no small feat, since numerals are deemed to express some of the most abstract thoughts our minds are able to conceive. After all, "two" does not exist in nature, but only groups of two concrete items, such as two fingers, two people, two sheep, two fruit, two leaves, or even sets of heterogeneous items such as one fruit + one leaf. "Two" is the abstraction of the quality of twoness shared by such sets.

The accountants of Uruk IVa can be credited with creating numerals and, in doing so, with revolutionizing accounting and data manipulation. In fact, the Uruk IVa accountants devised two types of signs: *numerals* (symbols encoding abstract numbers) and *pictographs* (signs expressing commodities). Each type of sign was traced in a different technique. Thus, pictographs were *incised*, whereas numerals were *impressed*, clearly standing out from the text. A tablet from Uruk, for example, features two accounts of "5 sheep" — shown by the pictograph for "sheep" (a circle with a cross) together with five impressed wedges representing "5" (fig. 32). The notion of number was finally dissociated from that of commodity.

The numerals of the Uruk IVa tablets constitute the first evidence for the use of abstract counting. The invention of numerals is of an importance equal to or greater than the invention of zero. Even if the notion of "nothing" was well understood by the Babylonians, the creation of a sign "0" in India about A.D. 700 changed the course of mathematics. Numerals and zero represent stages of abstraction which enabled humans to manipulate and process a greater volume of information and gain a new grasp of reality.

Fig. 32. Tablet showing accounts of sheep, Uruk, Iraq. Courtesy Vorderasiatisches Museum, Staatliche Museen zu Berlin.

Of course, we shall never know exactly where, when, how, and by whom abstract counting was invented, but the event seems to coincide with the change from tokens to writing for the simple reason that people would not use a counting device which had become obsolete.

The first numerals were not symbols specifically created in order to represent abstract numbers. Instead, they were the impressed signs, formerly indicating measures of grain, endowed with a new numerical value. The wedge, which originally meant a small quantity of grain, now stood for 1; the circle, which represented a larger quantity of grain, was 10; the large wedge, punched wedge, and large circle, which stood for still larger units of grain, were greater numbers as follows:

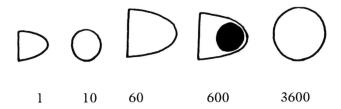

| 1 | 10 | 60 | 600 | 3600 |

It is also likely that the impressed units of animal numeration also served as numerals. The long wedge stood for 1; the circular marking, corresponding to the former lenticular disk, was 10. The animal numeration thus probably produced two units of the Sumerian arithmetical system, 1 and 10:

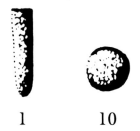

| 1 | 10 |

The preponderant role of plain tokens in prehistory was therefore perpetuated by the role of numerals in historical times. The mixed decimal-sexagesimal Sumerian counting system, which has puzzled many, probably derived from the plain tokens. For example, Friberg notes that, on the same tablet, the circular sign may stand alternatively in the ratio 1:6 or 1:10, depending upon what is being counted.[29] It is likely that "6" derives from the former unit of grain metrology (the sphere) and "10" from the unit of animal numeration (the lenticular disk). Animals were apparently counted by tens, probably using the fingers. On the other hand, 60 was particularly convenient for grain metrology, having the unique property of being divisible by 1, 2, 3, 4, 5, 6, 10, 12, 15 etc.[30]

In fact, the impressed signs, which came to represent numerals, never lost their primary meaning. Instead, according to the context, they had either an abstract or a concrete value. For example, a wedge preceding a pictograph was read "1"; alone, however, it stood for a measure of grain.

Abstract numbers, then, derived from the plain cones, spheres, cylinders, and lenticular disks that constituted the most ancient tokens. The reason why these particular symbols became the first numerals can only be hypothesized. David E. Smith has remarked that, in a number of societies, the words for expressing numbers derived from concrete numerations of particularly frequent use. He cites languages that expressed "one, two, three" by number words that meant literally "one grain, two grains, three grains," or "one stone, two stones, three stones" or, like the Niues of the southern Pacific, "one fruit, two fruit, three fruit."[31] It may be argued, therefore, that the first Sumerian abstract numbers derived from the grain and animal numerations because they were the most commonly used numerations in Mesopotamia. Grain, in particular, was not only the main staple but also the most common medium of exchange. Furthermore, grain metrology constituted a unique range of signs of increasing magnitude which could be easily converted to signify units of abstract counting such as 1, 6, 60, 180.

It was a major break with the past that pictographs encoding commodities were no longer repeated as many times as the number of units involved. Yet the invention of numerals did not put an end to the archaic principle of one-to-one correspondence, which continued to govern the use of numerals. "Nine" was represented by nine wedges, "fifty" by five circles, and so on. For instance, the tablet of Godin Tepe bearing the notation "33 jars of oil" displayed a single pictograph standing for "jar of oil" and expressed "33" by means of three impressed circles (10 + 10 + 10) and three wedges (1 + 1 + 1)(fig. 33). This archaism, in turn, was perpetuated for centuries in the Sumero-Babylonian arithmetical system. In fact, one-to-one correspondence persisted in all numbering systems, including those of Greece and Rome, until the invention of "arabic numerals" in India during the first millennium of our era.

Pictographic and Phonetic Writing
It was not by chance that the invention of pictography and phonetic writing coincided with that of numerals: both were the result of abstract counting.

Fig. 33. Incised tablet showing an account of thirty-three jars of oil(?), Godin Tepe (Gd 73–295), Iran. Courtesy T. Cuyler Young, Jr.

The abstraction of the concept of quantity (how many) from that of the quality of the item counted — concepts that were merged inextricably in the tokens — made possible the beginning of writing. Once dissociated from any notion of number, the pictographs could evolve in their own separate way. Symbols formerly used for keeping accounts of goods could expand to communicate any subject of human endeavor. As a result, things such as "the head of a man" or "mouth" — items which never had a token — were expressed by a picture. True pictography, wherein concepts were represented by their images, was an outcome of abstract counting.

After pictography, writing crossed several new thresholds about 3000 B.C., in the Uruk III period. The abstraction of quantity (how much) followed that of number (how many). Note, for example, that in Uruk VI (3500 B.C.) it took *one* token to indicate one jar of oil or, presumably, "one *sila* of oil." In Uruk IVa (3100 B.C.), the same idea was written with *two* signs: namely, "1" and the pictograph "*sila* of oil." In Uruk III, however (3000 B.C.), each notion ("1," "sila," and "oil") was expressed separately, requiring a sequence of *three* signs:

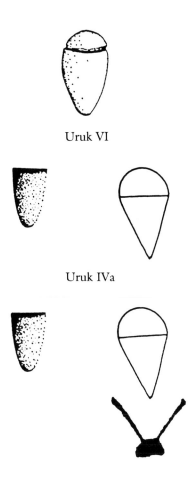

Uruk VI

Uruk IVa

Uruk III

Finally, symbols could function phonetically, representing sounds rather than objects. The incentive to resort to phonetics seems to have been prompted by new administrative requirements for recording the name of donors/recipients of goods on the tablets. Individuals' names were transcribed by symbols meant to be read phonetically as a rebus. The proper name Enlil-Ti, "Enlil (Gives) Life," was rendered by two pictographs: "god" (a star) and "life" (an arrow).[32] This was the point of departure for a syllabary—symbols standing not for commodities or concepts, but simply for the sounds they brought to mind. Pictography led to a syllabary, which was the true takeoff of writing.

IN THE ANCIENT NEAR EAST, writing emerged from a counting device. About 8000 B.C., tallying in one-to-one correspondence was superseded by tokens of many shapes suited for concrete counting. Finally, writing emerged as the main outcome of abstract counting, taking off when abstract counting dissociated the concept of numbers from that of the commodity accounted. Each change of reckoning device—tallies, plain tokens, complex tokens—corresponded to a new form of economy: hunting and gathering, agriculture, industry. Each change of reckoning device also corresponded to a new political system: egalitarian society, rank society, the state. Pictographic and phonetic writing, however, ca. 3100–3000 B.C., was independent of any socioeconomic event. It was the outcome of a new threshold in cognitive development—abstract counting.

Conclusions: Tokens, Their Role in Prehistory and Their Contribution to Archaeology

Writing appeared in the history of humanity some three or four thousand years before the beginning of our era, at a time when humanity had already made its most essential and fundamental discoveries . . . agriculture, the domestication of animals, pottery-making, weaving — a whole range of processes which were to allow human beings to stop living from day to day as they had done in paleolithic times, when they depended on hunting or the gathering of fruit, and to accumulate. . . . We must never lose sight of the fact that certain essential forms of progress, perhaps the most essential ever achieved by humanity, were accomplished without the help of writing.
— CLAUDE LÉVI-STRAUSS [1]

TOKENS ARE A UNIQUE SOURCE of information on important aspects of culture during five thousand years of Near Eastern prehistory, including two critical periods: the beginning of agriculture and the rise of cities. They offer insights into the economy, political structure, knowledge of mathematics, and means of communication in the societies that adopted them.

ECONOMY

The foremost function of tokens was to count goods. Plain tokens occurred concurrently with farming and served to count such agricultural products as animals and quantities of cereal. Complex tokens coincided with industry, keeping track of products for which Mesopotamia was famous: textiles and garments; luxury goods, such as perfume, metal, and jewelry; manufactured goods, such as bread, oil, or trussed ducks.

The shift from plain to complex tokens implies that the evolution of the system was closely tied to economic change. In turn, the counters can disclose the resources of past communities. Plain tokens can be clues to the domestication of plants and animals. Cylinders, used to count small cattle, can provide some notion of animal husbandry before osteological changes are noticeable, since it takes generations of domestication to alter an animal's bone structure. Complex tokens can identify the development of workshops.

POLITICAL STRUCTURE

The two stages of the token system, plain and complex, correspond to two phases in the evolution of social structure. Plain tokens served to pool resources in early farming communities. They imply a rank society. Complex tokens played an essential role in the collection of the dues and tribute which sustained the first Mesopotamian city-states. They signal state formation in southern Mesopotamia. Furthermore, the geographic distribution of complex tokens in strategic administrative centers outlines the area controlled by the South Mesopotamian bureaucracy and tells us about its organization.

MATHEMATICS

The most significant information contributed by the tokens is in the realm of counting. A multiplicity of token shapes for the accounting of goods is evidence of an archaic form of counting called concrete counting. What is more, the tokens' chronology, outlined below, suggests a gradual evolution from concrete to abstract counting:

ca. 8000–3500 B.C.: Counters of multiple shapes indicate a system of concrete counting; each category of goods necessitated a special type of counter. For example, jars of oil were counted with ovoids, and measures of grain were counted with cones. Numbers were indicated in one-to-one correspondence: three ovoids = three jars of oil.

ca. 3500–3100 B.C.: Markings impressed in one-to-one correspondence on envelopes and tablets show that the notions of product and number were still fused together. This implies that concrete counting prevailed.

ca. 3100 B.C. (Uruk IVa): Numerals were invented. The item counted and the number were finally dissociated. Each notion was expressed by a special sign, and the goods counted were indicated with *incised pictographs*. These pictographs were no longer repeated in one-to-one correspondence. The number of units was shown by numerals expressing 1, 10, 60, and 360. These were the first symbols expressing numbers abstractly—that is to say, independently from the item counted. These first numerals consisted of *impressed signs* formerly used to indicate measures of grain and numbers of animals which, from then on, carried a new abstract meaning.

ca. 3100–2500 B.C.: Archaic numerations for counting various categories of items still lingered, showing that the transition from concrete to abstract counting lasted for several centuries.

COMMUNICATION

The tokens were part of a chain of breakthroughs in communication. The first stage was the creation of the earliest known code, made possible by a conceptual leap: the creation of a set of tokens with specific shapes and the endowment of each shape with a unique, discrete meaning. The symbols were modeled in striking, distinct geometric shapes that were easy to recognize. The forms were simple and easy to duplicate, and the counters were systematically repeated, always carrying the same meaning. Later, with the development of a repertory of markings, the code grew to hundreds of concept signs. The system made it possible to deal concurrently with multiple kinds of data, thus allowing the processing and communication of a volume and complexity of information never reached previously.

The events that followed the invention of tokens can be reconstructed as follows:

> ca. 3700–2600 B.C.: A second stage was reached when groups of tokens representing particular transactions were enclosed in envelopes to be kept in archives. Some envelopes bore on the outside the impression of the tokens held inside. Such markings on envelopes were the turning point between tokens and writing.
>
> ca. 3500–3100 B.C. (starting in Uruk VI–V): Tablets displaying impressed markings in the shape of tokens superseded the envelopes.
>
> ca. 3100–3000 B.C. (starting in Uruk IVa): Pictographic script traced with a stylus on clay tablets marked the true takeoff of writing. The tokens dwindled.

We have seen that when two concepts—namely, "numbers" and "items counted"—were abstracted, the pictographs were no longer confined to indicating numbers of units of goods. With the invention of numerals, pictography was no longer restricted to accounting but could encompass other fields of human endeavor. From then on, writing could become phonetic and develop into the versatile tool that it is today, able to store and convey any possible idea. The invention of abstract numerals was the beginning of mathematics; it was also the beginning of writing.

The tokens were mundane counters dealing with foods and other basic commodities of daily life, but they played a major role in the societies that adopted them. They were used to manage goods and they affected the economy; they were an instrument of power and they created new social patterns; they were employed for data manipulation and they changed a mode of thought. Above all, the tokens were a counting and record-keeping device and were the watershed of mathematics and communication.

DRAWINGS AND PHOTOGRAPHS

One representative example of each subtype of token was selected for the following charts. It is important to realize, though, that because the tokens were manufactured by hand, they are not standardized. The photographic catalog in *Before Writing, Volume II: A Catalog of Near Eastern Tokens* illustrates how artifacts of the same subtype show slight variations in form and style of markings (for example, type 6: 14 or 8: 17). Several drawings of the same subtype are provided only when major variations occur (for example, differences in profile in type 3: 51). The various painted patterns on cones (type 1: 46) or disks (type 3: 79) are not illustrated.

Perforated, rather than unperforated, artifacts have been selected for illustration in order to show the place of the perforations. When warranted, several drawings depict variations in the placement of perforations (for example, in type 3: 19).

Whenever possible, the drawings were based on photographs. In many instances, however, the only sources available to the artist were sketches from notes taken in museums. The scale could not be taken into account in the illustrations. The key to the drawings follows:

Perforation

Punctation

Incised line

Painted motif

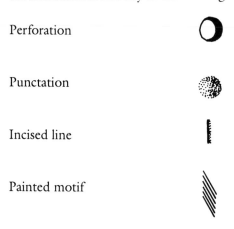

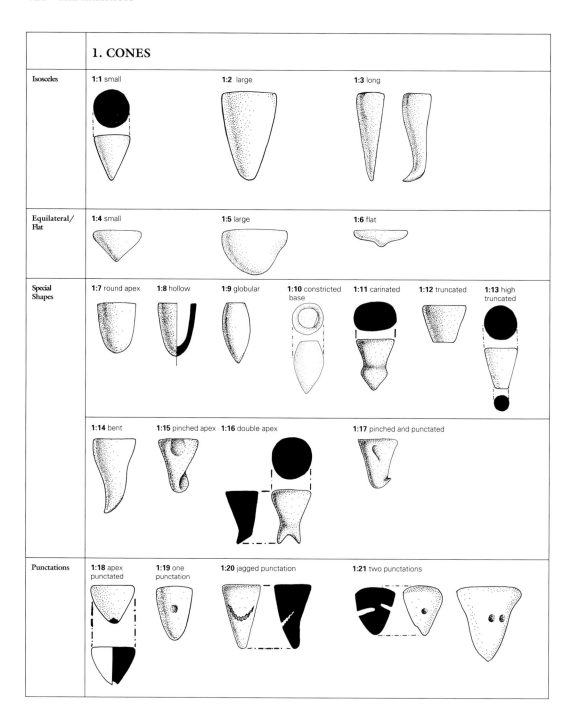

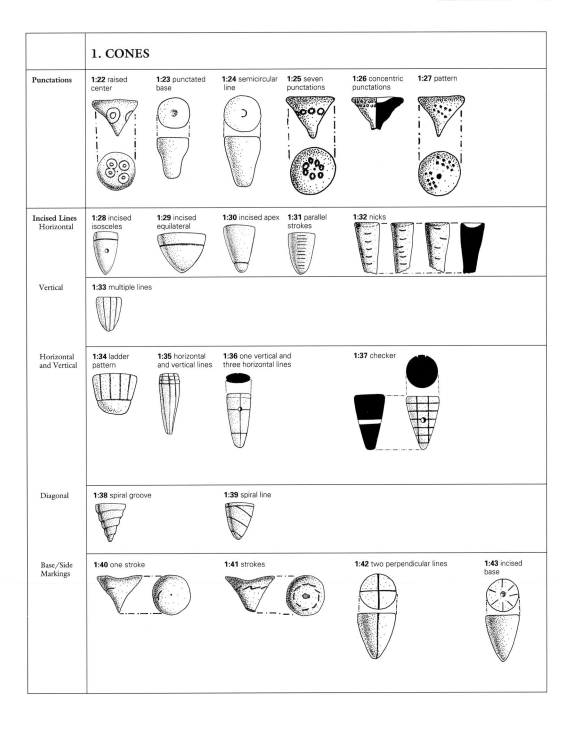

1. CONES

Punctations

1:22 raised center **1:23** punctated base **1:24** semicircular line **1:25** seven punctations **1:26** concentric punctations **1:27** pattern

Incised Lines
Horizontal

1:28 incised isosceles **1:29** incised equilateral **1:30** incised apex **1:31** parallel strokes **1:32** nicks

Vertical

1:33 multiple lines

Horizontal and Vertical

1:34 ladder pattern **1:35** horizontal and vertical lines **1:36** one vertical and three horizontal lines **1:37** checker

Diagonal

1:38 spiral groove **1:39** spiral line

Base/Side Markings

1:40 one stroke **1:41** strokes **1:42** two perpendicular lines **1:43** incised base

1. CONES

Incised Lines Patterns	**1:44** St. Andrew's cross **1:45** dotted triangles
Painted	**1:46** painted
Appliqué Markings	**1:47** appliqué pebble **1:48** appliqué pellet **1:49** appliqué coil

2. SPHERES

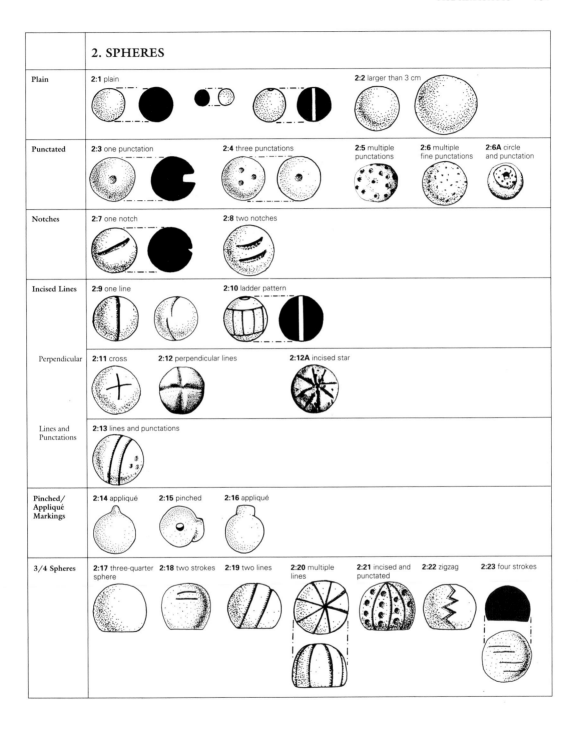

Plain	2:1 plain 2:2 larger than 3 cm
Punctated	2:3 one punctation 2:4 three punctations 2:5 multiple punctations 2:6 multiple fine punctations 2:6A circle and punctation
Notches	2:7 one notch 2:8 two notches
Incised Lines	2:9 one line 2:10 ladder pattern
Perpendicular	2:11 cross 2:12 perpendicular lines 2:12A incised star
Lines and Punctations	2:13 lines and punctations
Pinched/ Appliqué Markings	2:14 appliqué 2:15 pinched 2:16 appliqué
3/4 Spheres	2:17 three-quarter sphere 2:18 two strokes 2:19 two lines 2:20 multiple lines 2:21 incised and punctated 2:22 zigzag 2:23 four strokes

2. SPHERES

1/2 Spheres	**2:24** half sphere	**2:25** one line	**2:26** one groove	**2:27** strokes	**2:27A** one punctation	**2:28** multiple punctations	**2:29** pinched

1/4 Spheres	**2:30** one-quarter sphere **2:31** one stroke **2:32** two strokes **2:33** multiple strokes

3. DISKS

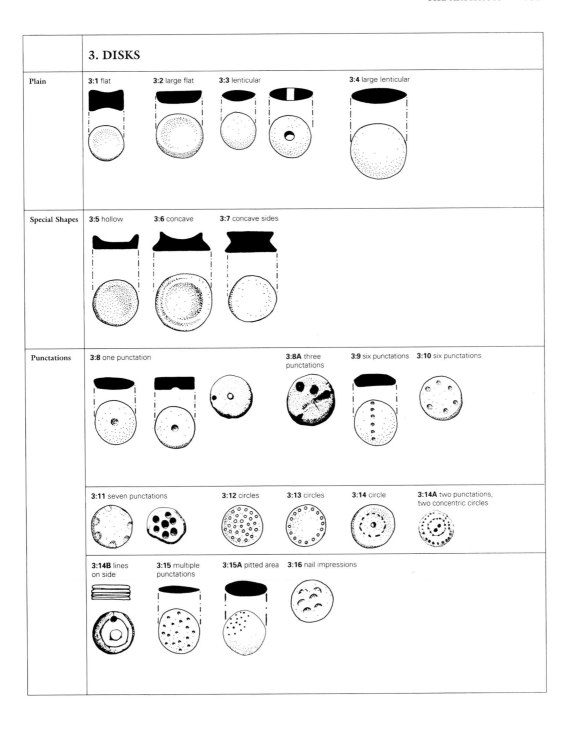

Plain	**3:1** flat	**3:2** large flat	**3:3** lenticular		**3:4** large lenticular

Special Shapes	**3:5** hollow	**3:6** concave	**3:7** concave sides

Punctations	**3:8** one punctation			**3:8A** three punctations	**3:9** six punctations	**3:10** six punctations

3:11 seven punctations   **3:12** circles   **3:13** circles   **3:14** circle   **3:14A** two punctations, two concentric circles

3:14B lines on side   **3:15** multiple punctations   **3:15A** pitted area   **3:16** nail impressions

3. DISKS

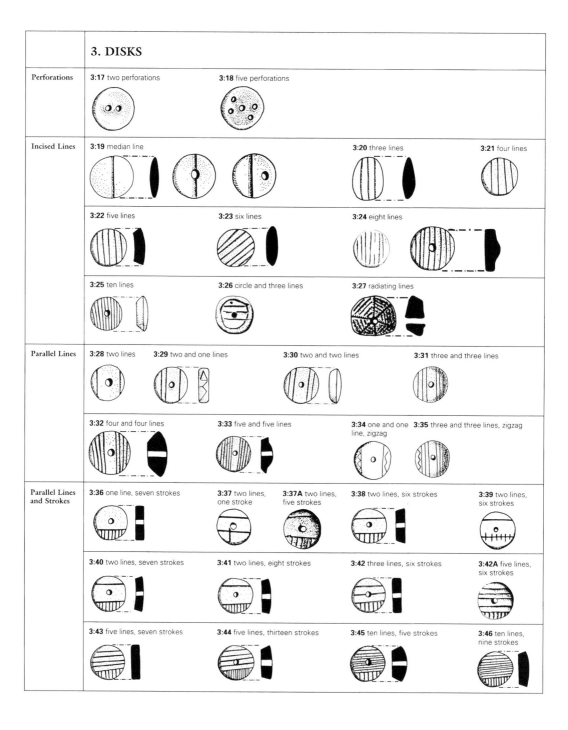

Perforations	**3:17** two perforations **3:18** five perforations
Incised Lines	**3:19** median line **3:20** three lines **3:21** four lines **3:22** five lines **3:23** six lines **3:24** eight lines **3:25** ten lines **3:26** circle and three lines **3:27** radiating lines
Parallel Lines	**3:28** two lines **3:29** two and one lines **3:30** two and two lines **3:31** three and three lines **3:32** four and four lines **3:33** five and five lines **3:34** one and one **3:35** three and three lines, zigzag line, zigzag
Parallel Lines and Strokes	**3:36** one line, seven strokes **3:37** two lines, one stroke **3:37A** two lines, five strokes **3:38** two lines, six strokes **3:39** two lines, six strokes **3:40** two lines, seven strokes **3:41** two lines, eight strokes **3:42** three lines, six strokes **3:42A** five lines, six strokes **3:43** five lines, seven strokes **3:44** five lines, thirteen strokes **3:45** ten lines, five strokes **3:46** ten lines, nine strokes

3. DISKS

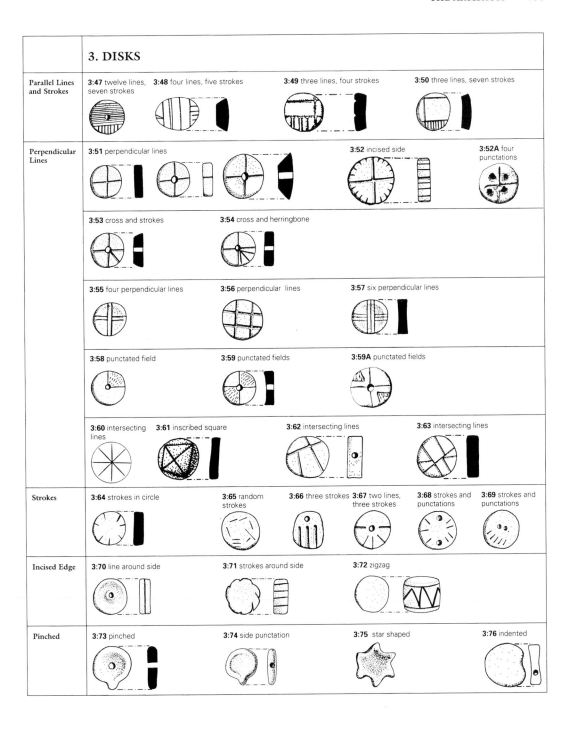

Parallel Lines and Strokes

3:47 twelve lines, seven strokes   3:48 four lines, five strokes   3:49 three lines, four strokes   3:50 three lines, seven strokes

Perpendicular Lines

3:51 perpendicular lines   3:52 incised side   3:52A four punctations

3:53 cross and strokes   3:54 cross and herringbone

3:55 four perpendicular lines   3:56 perpendicular lines   3:57 six perpendicular lines

3:58 punctated field   3:59 punctated fields   3:59A punctated fields

3:60 intersecting lines   3:61 inscribed square   3:62 intersecting lines   3:63 intersecting lines

Strokes

3:64 strokes in circle   3:65 random strokes   3:66 three strokes   3:67 two lines, three strokes   3:68 strokes and punctations   3:69 strokes and punctations

Incised Edge

3:70 line around side   3:71 strokes around side   3:72 zigzag

Pinched

3:73 pinched   3:74 side punctation   3:75 star shaped   3:76 indented

3. DISKS

Pinched	**3:77** indented	**3:78** folded over
Painted	**3:79** painted	**3:80** painted cross
High	**3:81** high **3:82** punctation **3:83** perpendicular lines	
Reworked Sherds	**3:84** reworked sherd	**3:85** reworked painted sherd
Pebbles	**3:86** pebble	**3:87** incised pebble

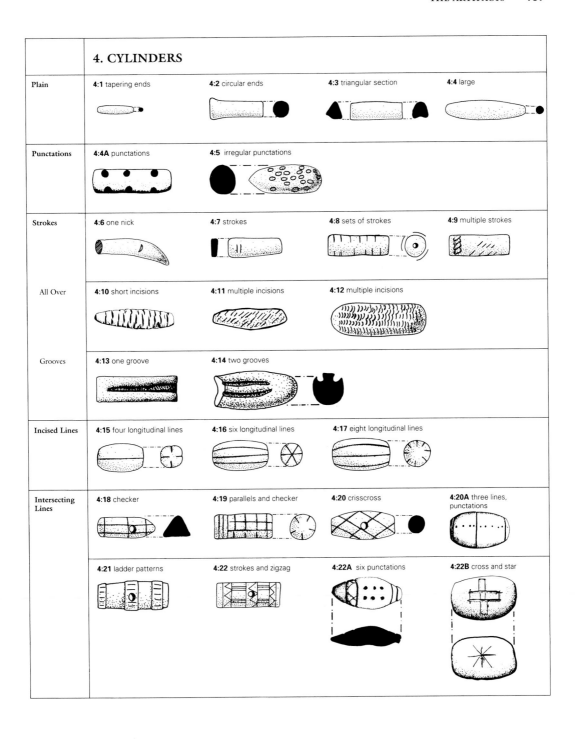

4. CYLINDERS

Plain

4:1 tapering ends   **4:2** circular ends   **4:3** triangular section   **4:4** large

Punctations

4:4A punctations   **4:5** irregular punctations

Strokes

4:6 one nick   **4:7** strokes   **4:8** sets of strokes   **4:9** multiple strokes

All Over

4:10 short incisions   **4:11** multiple incisions   **4:12** multiple incisions

Grooves

4:13 one groove   **4:14** two grooves

Incised Lines

4:15 four longitudinal lines   **4:16** six longitudinal lines   **4:17** eight longitudinal lines

Intersecting Lines

4:18 checker   **4:19** parallels and checker   **4:20** crisscross   **4:20A** three lines, punctations

4:21 ladder patterns   **4:22** strokes and zigzag   **4:22A** six punctations   **4:22B** cross and star

4. CYLINDERS

Intersecting Lines Diagonal Lines	**4:23** circular lines	**4:24** crisscross	
Painted	**4:25** painted	**4:26** painted lines	
Pinched/ Appliqué	**4:27** pinched	**4:28** median constriction	**4:29** appliqué coils
Modeled Twisted	**4:30** decreasing section	**4:31** hand squeezed	**4:32** twisted

5. TETRAHEDRONS

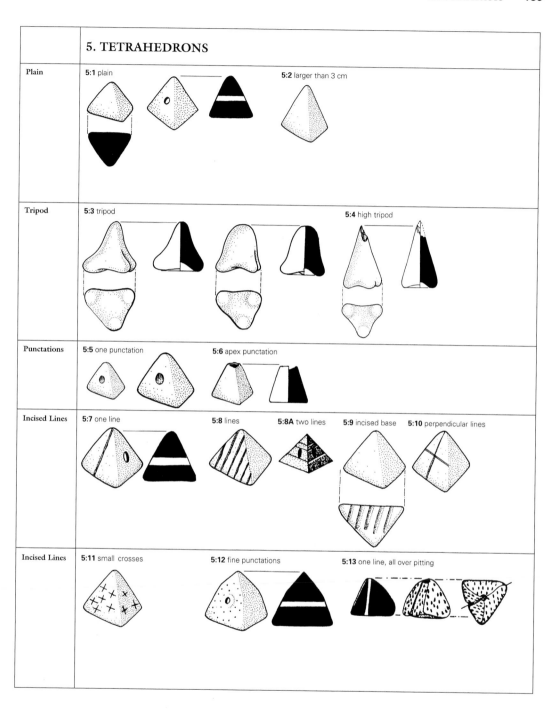

Plain

5:1 plain   **5:2** larger than 3 cm

Tripod

5:3 tripod   **5:4** high tripod

Punctations

5:5 one punctation   **5:6** apex punctation

Incised Lines

5:7 one line   **5:8** lines   **5:8A** two lines   **5:9** incised base   **5:10** perpendicular lines

Incised Lines

5:11 small crosses   **5:12** fine punctations   **5:13** one line, all over pitting

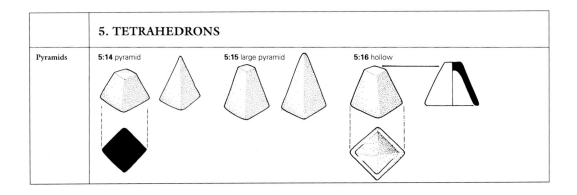

Pyramids	**5. TETRAHEDRONS**		
	5:14 pyramid	**5:15** large pyramid	**5:16** hollow

6. OVOIDS

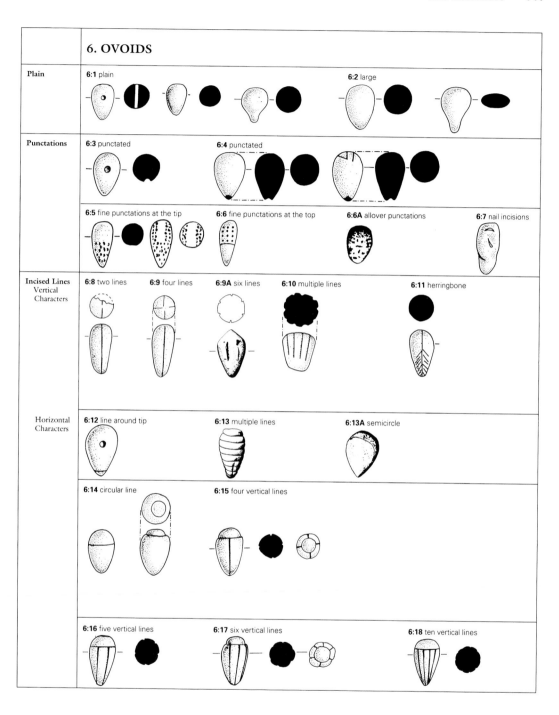

Plain

6:1 plain   **6:2** large

Punctations

6:3 punctated   **6:4** punctated

6:5 fine punctations at the tip   **6:6** fine punctations at the top   **6:6A** allover punctations   **6:7** nail incisions

Incised Lines
Vertical
Characters

6:8 two lines   **6:9** four lines   **6:9A** six lines   **6:10** multiple lines   **6:11** herringbone

Horizontal
Characters

6:12 line around tip   **6:13** multiple lines   **6:13A** semicircle

6:14 circular line   **6:15** four vertical lines

6:16 five vertical lines   **6:17** six vertical lines   **6:18** ten vertical lines

	6. OVOIDS			
Incised Lines Horizontal Characters	**6:19** cross	**6:20** herringbone **6:21** incised and punctated		**6:22** six punctations
Intersecting Characters	**6:23** cross	**6:24** two diagonal lines and cross	**6:25** crisscross	
Pinched/ Appliqué	**6:26** pinched	**6:27** appliqué coil	**6:28** appliqué pellets	

7. QUADRANGLES

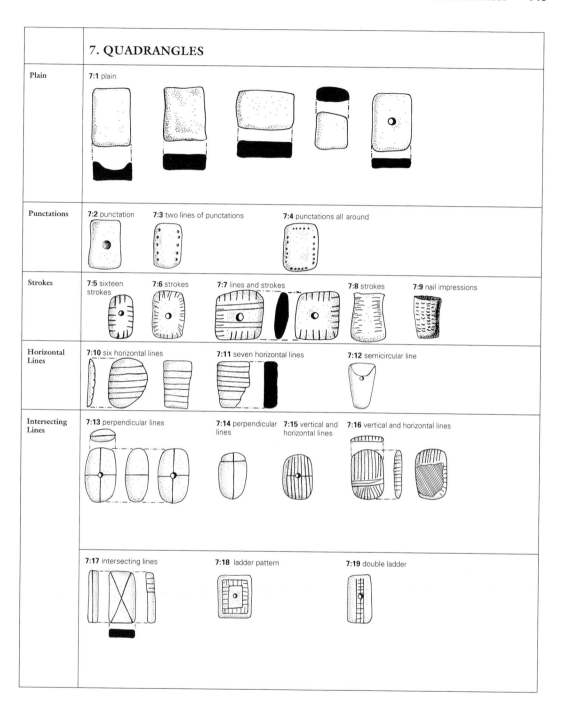

Plain	**7:1** plain
Punctations	**7:2** punctation **7:3** two lines of punctations **7:4** punctations all around
Strokes	**7:5** sixteen strokes **7:6** strokes **7:7** lines and strokes **7:8** strokes **7:9** nail impressions
Horizontal Lines	**7:10** six horizontal lines **7:11** seven horizontal lines **7:12** semicircular line
Intersecting Lines	**7:13** perpendicular lines **7:14** perpendicular lines **7:15** vertical and horizontal lines **7:16** vertical and horizontal lines **7:17** intersecting lines **7:18** ladder pattern **7:19** double ladder

7. QUADRANGLES

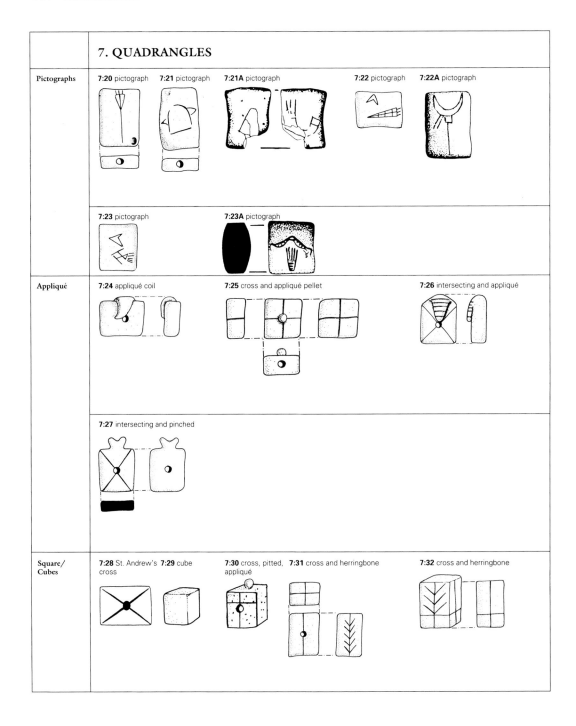

Pictographs

7:20 pictograph **7:21** pictograph **7:21A** pictograph **7:22** pictograph **7:22A** pictograph

7:23 pictograph **7:23A** pictograph

Appliqué

7:24 appliqué coil **7:25** cross and appliqué pellet **7:26** intersecting and appliqué

7:27 intersecting and pinched

Square/ Cubes

7:28 St. Andrew's **7:29** cube cross **7:30** cross, pitted, **7:31** cross and herringbone appliqué **7:32** cross and herringbone

8. TRIANGLES

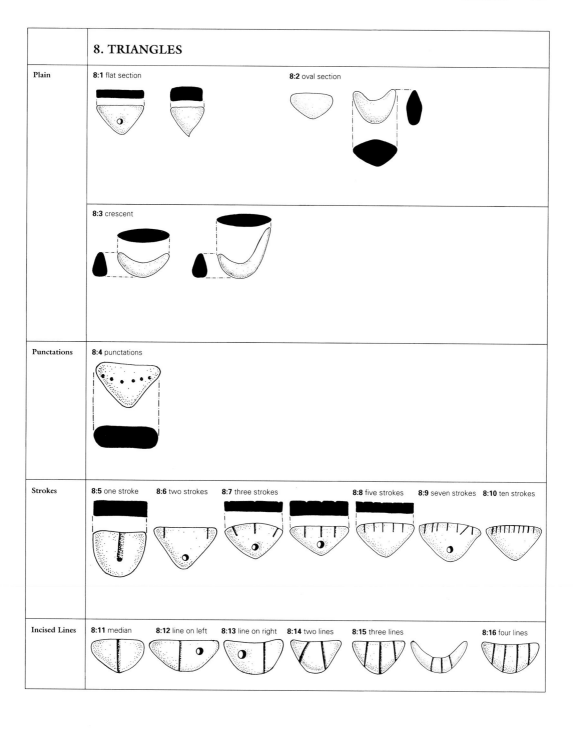

Plain

8:1 flat section   **8:2** oval section

8:3 crescent

Punctations

8:4 punctations

Strokes

8:5 one stroke   **8:6** two strokes   **8:7** three strokes   **8:8** five strokes   **8:9** seven strokes   **8:10** ten strokes

Incised Lines

8:11 median   **8:12** line on left   **8:13** line on right   **8:14** two lines   **8:15** three lines   **8:16** four lines

8. TRIANGLES

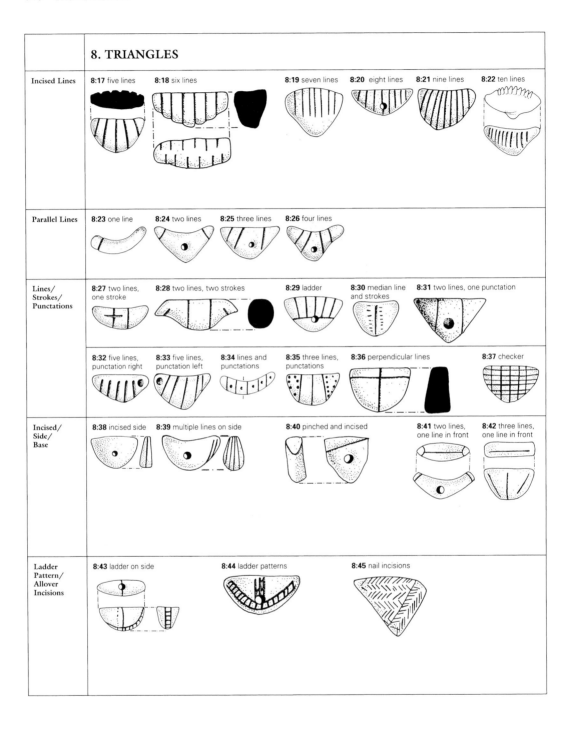

Incised Lines	**8:17** five lines **8:18** six lines **8:19** seven lines **8:20** eight lines **8:21** nine lines **8:22** ten lines
Parallel Lines	**8:23** one line **8:24** two lines **8:25** three lines **8:26** four lines
Lines/ Strokes/ Punctations	**8:27** two lines, one stroke **8:28** two lines, two strokes **8:29** ladder **8:30** median line and strokes **8:31** two lines, one punctation **8:32** five lines, punctation right **8:33** five lines, punctation left **8:34** lines and punctations **8:35** three lines, punctations **8:36** perpendicular lines **8:37** checker
Incised/ Side/ Base	**8:38** incised side **8:39** multiple lines on side **8:40** pinched and incised **8:41** two lines, one line in front **8:42** three lines, one line in front
Ladder Pattern/ Allover Incisions	**8:43** ladder on side **8:44** ladder patterns **8:45** nail incisions

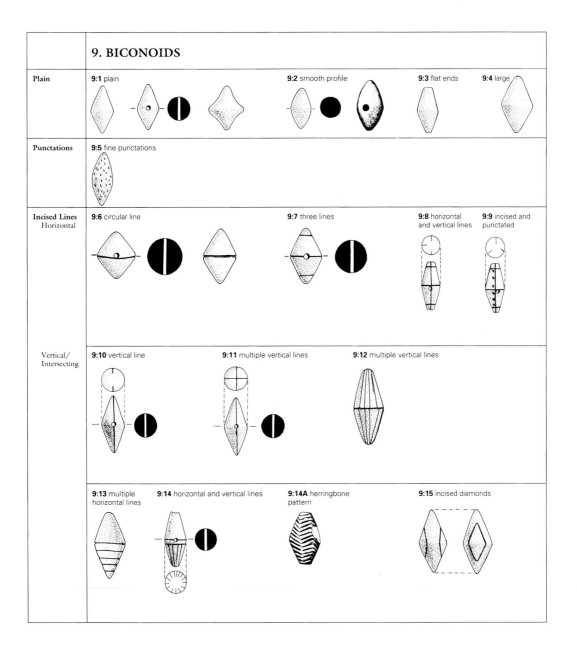

9. BICONOIDS

Plain

9:1 plain   **9:2** smooth profile   **9:3** flat ends   **9:4** large

Punctations

9:5 fine punctations

Incised Lines
Horizontal

9:6 circular line   **9:7** three lines   **9:8** horizontal and vertical lines   **9:9** incised and punctated

Vertical/ Intersecting

9:10 vertical line   **9:11** multiple vertical lines   **9:12** multiple vertical lines

9:13 multiple horizontal lines   **9:14** horizontal and vertical lines   **9:14A** herringbone pattern   **9:15** incised diamonds

10. PARABOLOIDS

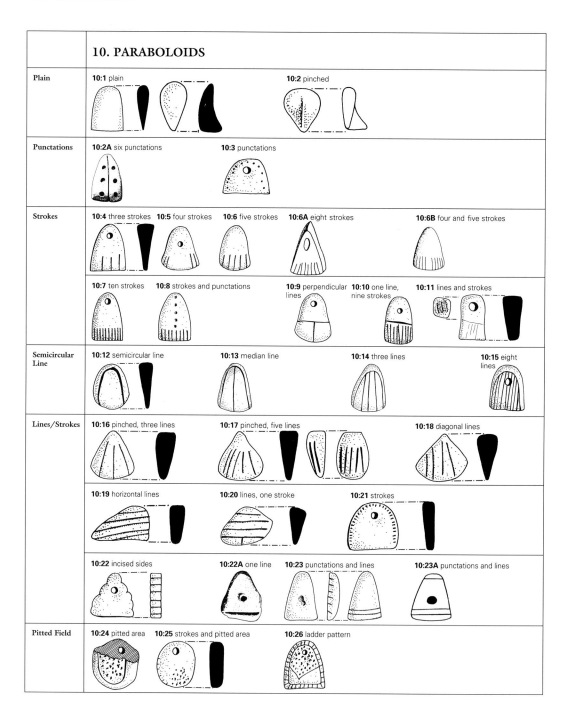

Plain	10:1 plain 10:2 pinched
Punctations	10:2A six punctations 10:3 punctations
Strokes	10:4 three strokes 10:5 four strokes 10:6 five strokes 10:6A eight strokes 10:6B four and five strokes
	10:7 ten strokes 10:8 strokes and punctations 10:9 perpendicular lines 10:10 one line, nine strokes 10:11 lines and strokes
Semicircular Line	10:12 semicircular line 10:13 median line 10:14 three lines 10:15 eight lines
Lines/Strokes	10:16 pinched, three lines 10:17 pinched, five lines 10:18 diagonal lines
	10:19 horizontal lines 10:20 lines, one stroke 10:21 strokes
	10:22 incised sides 10:22A one line 10:23 punctations and lines 10:23A punctations and lines
Pitted Field	10:24 pitted area 10:25 strokes and pitted area 10:26 ladder pattern

11. BENT COILS

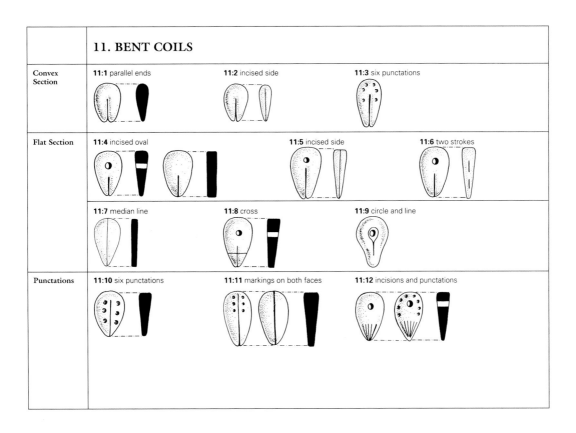

Convex Section	**11:1** parallel ends **11:2** incised side **11:3** six punctations
Flat Section	**11:4** incised oval **11:5** incised side **11:6** two strokes
	11:7 median line **11:8** cross **11:9** circle and line
Punctations	**11:10** six punctations **11:11** markings on both faces **11:12** incisions and punctations

12. OVALS/RHOMBOIDS

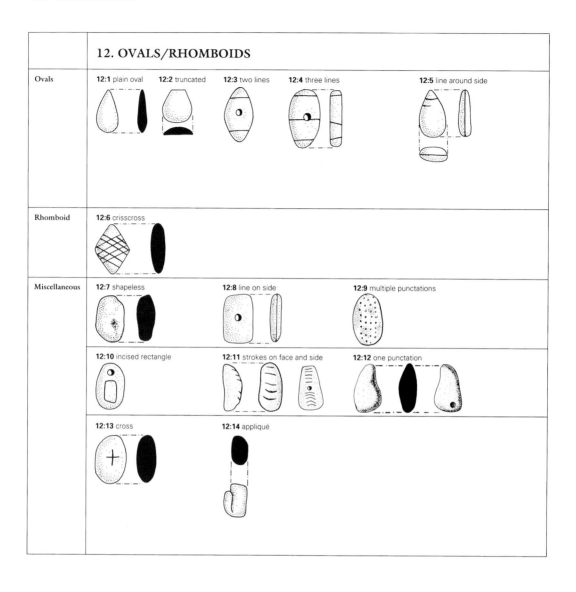

Ovals

12:1 plain oval   **12:2** truncated   **12:3** two lines   **12:4** three lines   **12:5** line around side

Rhomboid

12:6 crisscross

Miscellaneous

12:7 shapeless   **12:8** line on side   **12:9** multiple punctations

12:10 incised rectangle   **12:11** strokes on face and side   **12:12** one punctation

12:13 cross   **12:14** appliqué

13. VESSELS

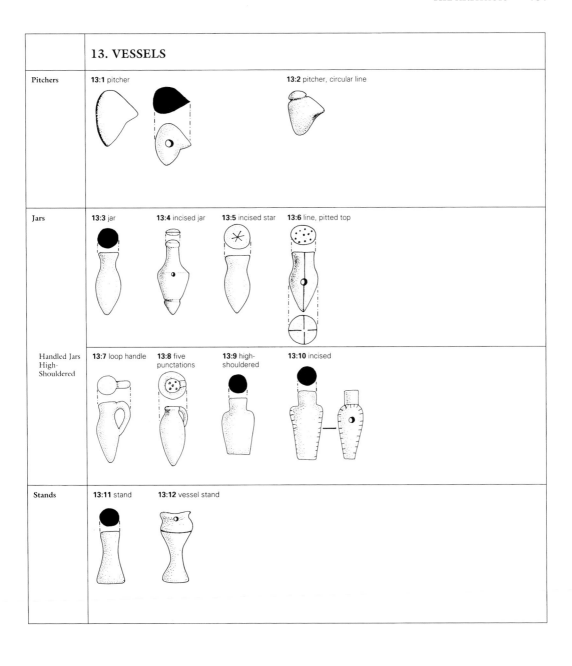

Pitchers

13:1 pitcher

13:2 pitcher, circular line

Jars

13:3 jar

13:4 incised jar

13:5 incised star

13:6 line, pitted top

Handled Jars High-Shouldered

13:7 loop handle

13:8 five punctations

13:9 high-shouldered

13:10 incised

Stands

13:11 stand

13:12 vessel stand

13. VESSELS

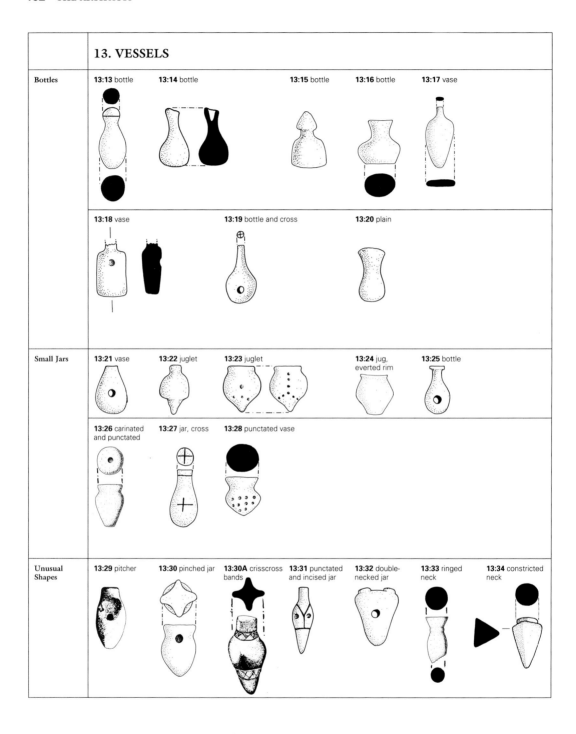

Bottles

13:13 bottle **13:14** bottle **13:15** bottle **13:16** bottle **13:17** vase

13:18 vase **13:19** bottle and cross **13:20** plain

Small Jars

13:21 vase **13:22** juglet **13:23** juglet **13:24** jug, everted rim **13:25** bottle

13:26 carinated and punctated **13:27** jar, cross **13:28** punctated vase

Unusual Shapes

13:29 pitcher **13:30** pinched jar **13:30A** crisscross bands **13:31** punctated and incised jar **13:32** double-necked jar **13:33** ringed neck **13:34** constricted neck

13. VESSELS

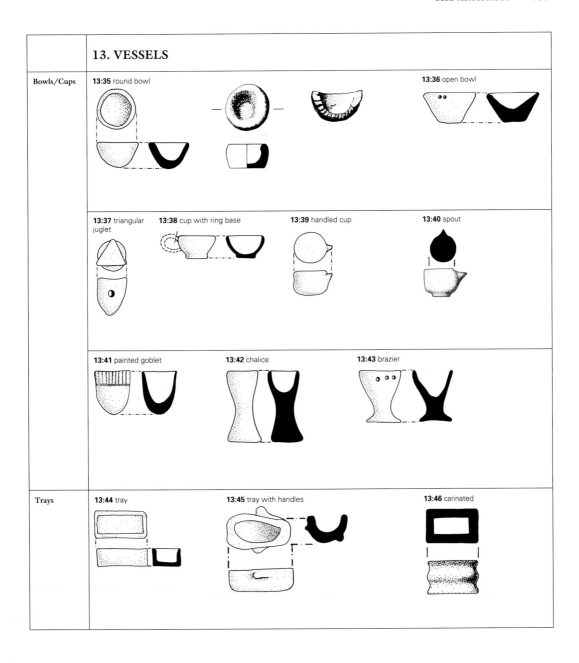

Bowls/Cups

13:35 round bowl

13:36 open bowl

13:37 triangular juglet

13:38 cup with ring base

13:39 handled cup

13:40 spout

13:41 painted goblet

13:42 chalice

13:43 brazier

Trays

13:44 tray

13:45 tray with handles

13:46 carinated

14. TOOLS

Tools			
	14:1 axe shaped	**14:2** hoe shaped	**14:3** hoe shaped
	14:4 spade	**14:5** axe shaped	**14:6** saw shaped
	14:7 sickle shaped	**14:8** tool	**14:9** saw-toothed
Furniture/ Utensils	**14:10** bed	**14:11** ladle	

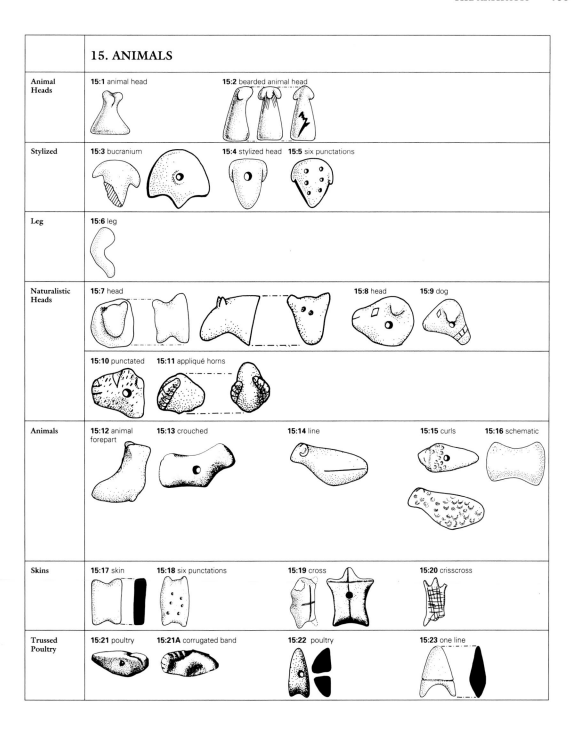

15. ANIMALS

Animal Heads	**15:1** animal head **15:2** bearded animal head
Stylized	**15:3** bucranium **15:4** stylized head **15:5** six punctations
Leg	**15:6** leg
Naturalistic Heads	**15:7** head **15:8** head **15:9** dog **15:10** punctated **15:11** appliqué horns
Animals	**15:12** animal forepart **15:13** crouched **15:14** line **15:15** curls **15:16** schematic
Skins	**15:17** skin **15:18** six punctations **15:19** cross **15:20** crisscross
Trussed Poultry	**15:21** poultry **15:21A** corrugated band **15:22** poultry **15:23** one line

15. ANIMALS

Trussed Poultry	

15:24 trussed duck

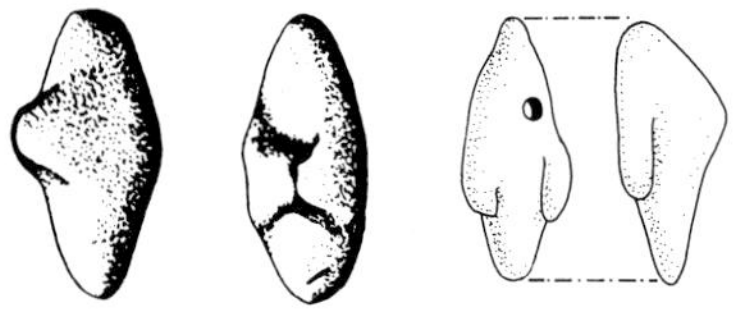

15:25 trussed duck

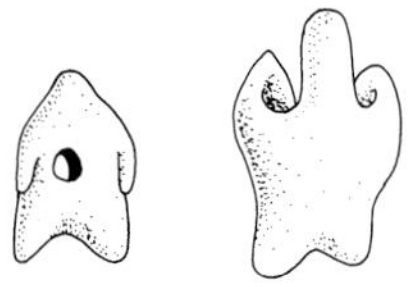

15:26 three lines

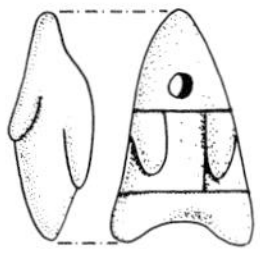

15:27 trussed duck

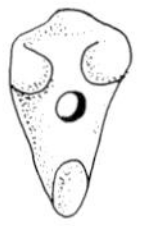

15:28 perpendicular lines

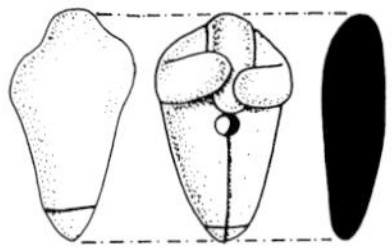

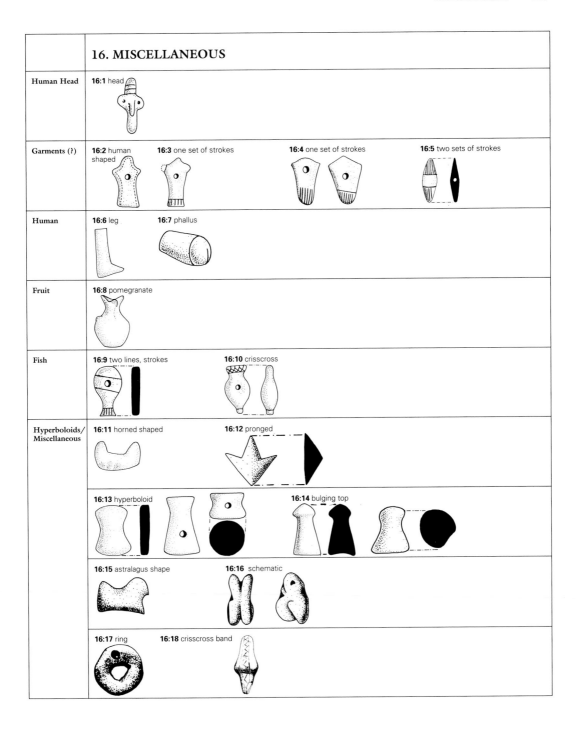

	16. MISCELLANEOUS
Human Head	16:1 head
Garments (?)	16:2 human shaped 16:3 one set of strokes 16:4 one set of strokes 16:5 two sets of strokes
Human	16:6 leg 16:7 phallus
Fruit	16:8 pomegranate
Fish	16:9 two lines, strokes 16:10 crisscross
Hyperboloids/ Miscellaneous	16:11 horned shaped 16:12 pronged
	16:13 hyperboloid 16:14 bulging top
	16:15 astralagus shape 16:16 schematic
	16:17 ring 16:18 crisscross band

Notes

ABBREVIATIONS

ATU   Adam Falkenstein, *Archaische Texte aus Uruk,* Ausgrabungen der deutschen Forschungsgemeinschaft in Uruk-Warka, vol. 2 (Leipzig: Kommissionsverlag Otto Harrassowitz, 1936).

BaM   *Baghdader Mitteilungen* (Berlin).

BW   Denise Schmandt-Besserat, *Before Writing, Volume I: From Counting to Cuneiform; Volume II: A Catalog of Near Eastern Tokens* (Austin: University of Texas Press, 1992).

Dafi 1a   Geneviève Dollfus, "Les Fouilles à Djaffarabad de 1969 à 1971," *Cahiers de la Délégation Archéologique Française en Iran,* vol. 1, 1971, pp. 17–161.

Dafi 1b   Alain Le Brun, "Recherches stratigraphiques à l'Acropole de Suse (1969–1971)," *Cahiers de la Délégation Archéologique Française en Iran,* vol. 1, 1971, pp. 163–216.

Dafi 1c   François Vallat, "Les documents épigraphiques de l'Acropole (1969–1971)," *Cahiers de la Délégation Archéologique Française en Iran,* vol. 1, 1971, pp. 235–245.

Dafi 3   François Vallat, "Les Tablettes proto-élamites de l'Acropole (Campagne 1972)," *Cahiers de la Délégation Archéologique Française en Iran,* vol. 3, 1973, pp. 93–103.

Dafi 5   Geneviève Dollfus, "Les Fouilles à Djaffarabad de 1972 à 1974, Djaffarabad, périodes I et II," *Cahiers de la Délégation Archéologique Française en Iran,* vol. 5, 1975, pp. 11–219.

Dafi 8a   Alain Le Brun and François Vallat, "L'Origine de l'écriture à Suse," *Cahiers de la Délégation Archéologique Française en Iran,* vol. 8, 1978, pp. 11–59.

Dafi 8b   Alain Le Brun, "La Glyptique du niveau 17B de l'Acropole (Campagne 1972)," *Cahiers de la Délégation Archéologique Française en Iran,* vol. 8, 1978, pp. 61–79.

Dafi 9a   Denis Canal, "La Terrase haute de l'Acropole de Suse," *Cahiers de la Délégation Française en Iran,* vol. 9, 1978, pp. 11–55.

Dafi 9b Alain Le Brun, "Le Niveau 17B de l'Acropole de Suse (Campagne 1972)," *Cahiers de la Délégation Archéologique Française en Iran*, vol. 9, 1978, pp. 57–154.

M 7 J. de Morgan, G. Jéquier, R. de Mecquenem, B. Haussoulier, and D.-L. Graat van Roggen, *Mémoires de la Délégation en Perse*, vol. 7, *Recherches archéologiques, 2ème série* (Paris: Editions Ernest Leroux, 1905).

M 12 M.-C. Soutzo, G. Pézard, G. Bondoux, R. de Mecquenem, M. Pézard, J.-E. Gautier, and P. Toscanne, *Mémoires de la Délégation en Perse*, vol. 12, *Recherches archéologiques, 4ème série* (Paris: Editions Ernest Leroux, 1911).

M 13 E. Pottier, J. de Morgan, and R. de Mecquenem, *Mémoires de la Délégation en Perse*, vol. 13, *Recherches archéologiques, 5ème série. Céramique peinte de Suse et petits monuments de l'époque archaïque* (Paris: Editions Ernest Leroux, 1912).

M 16 L. Legrain, *Mémoires de la Mission archéologique de Perse*, vol. 16, *Empreintes de cachets élamites* (Paris: Editions Ernest Leroux, 1921).

M 17 V. Scheil, *Mémoires de la Mission archéologique de Perse*, vol. 17, *Textes de comptabilité proto-élamites (nouvelle série)* (Paris: Editions Ernest Leroux, 1923).

M 25 Allote de la Fuye, N.-T. Belaiew, R. de Mecquenem, and J.-M. Unvala, *Mémoires de la Mission archéologique de Perse*, vol. 25, *Archéologie, métrologie et numismatique susiennes* (Paris: Editions Ernest Leroux, 1934).

M 29 R. de Mecquenem, G. Contenau, R. Pfister, and N. Belaiew, *Mémoires de la Mission archéologique en Iran, Mission de Susiane*, vol. 29, *Archéologie susienne* (Paris: Presses Universitaires de France, 1943).

M 30 R. de Mecquenem, G. Contenau, R. Pfister, and N. Belaiew, *Mémoires de la Mission archéologique en Iran, Mission de Susiane*, vol. 30, *Archéologie susienne* (Paris: Presses Universitaires de France, 1947).

M 43 Pierre Amiet, *Mémoires de la Délégation archéologique en Iran, Mission de Susiane*, vol. 43, *La Glyptique susienne*, vols. 1 and 2 (Paris: Librairie Orientaliste Paul Geuthner, 1972).

M 46 M. J. Steve and H. Gasche, *Mémoires de la Délégation archéologique en Iran, Mission de Susiane*, vol. 46, *L'Acropole de Suse* (Leiden: E. J. Brill; Paris: P. Geuthner, 1971).

OIC Oriental Institute Communications. Chicago: University of Chicago.

OIP Oriental Institute Publications. Chicago: University of Chicago.

PI S. Langdon, *The Herbert Weld Collection in the Ashmolean Museum: Pictographic Inscriptions from Jemdet Nasr*, Oxford Editions of Cuneiform Texts 7 (Oxford, 1928).

UVB Julius Jordan, *Vorläufiger Bericht über die von der deutschen Forschungsgemeinschaft in Uruk-Warka unternommenen Ausgrabungen, Abhandlungen der preussischen Akademie der Wissenschaften, Phil.-hist. Klasse* (Berlin), vol. 2, 1931; vol. 3, 1932.

Heinrich J. Lenzen, *Vorläufiger Bericht über die von dem deutschen archäologischen Institut und der deutschen Orientgesellschaft aus Mitteln der deutschen Forschungsgemeinschaft unternommenen Ausgrabungen in Uruk-Warka* (Berlin), vol. 15, 1959; vol. 17, 1961; vol. 21, 1965; vol. 22, 1966; vol. 23, 1967; vol. 24, 1968; vol. 25, 1974. Jürgen Schmidt, *Vorläufiger Bericht über die von dem deutschen archäologischen Institut aus Mitteln der deutschen Forschungsgemeinschaft unternommenen Ausgrabungen in Uruk-Warka* (Berlin), vols. 31 and 32, 1983.

ZATU M. W. Green and Hans J. Nissen, *Zeichenliste der archaischen Texte aus Uruk,* Ausgrabungen der deutschen Forschungsgemeinschaft in Uruk-Warka, vol. 11, *Archaische Texte aus Uruk,* vol. 2 (Berlin: Gebrüder Mann Verlag, 1987).

INTRODUCTION

1. Colin Cherry, *On Human Communication* (New York: John Wiley and Sons, 1957), p. 31.

2. Marvin A. Powell, "Three Problems in the History of Cuneiform Writing: Origins, Direction of Script, Literacy," *Visible Language* 15, no. 4 (1981): 419–420.

3. Ignace J. Gelb, *A Study of Writing* (Chicago: University of Chicago Press, 1974), p. 63.

4. Geoffrey Sampson, *Writing Systems* (Stanford, Calif.: Stanford University Press, 1985), pp. 46–47.

5. Donald Jackson, *The Story of Writing* (New York: Taplinger Publishing Company, 1981), pp. 16–17.

6. Géza Komoróczy, "Zur Ätiologie der Schrift Erfindung im Enmerkar Epos," *Altorientalische Forschungen* 3 (1975): 19–24; Sol Cohen, "Enmerkar and the Lord of Aratta," Ph.D. dissertation, University of Pennsylvania, 1973, pp. 26–40; Samuel Noah Kramer, *Enmerkar and the Lord of Aratta,* University Museum Monograph (Philadelphia: University of Pennsylvania, 1952), p. 2.

7. Cohen, "Enmerkar," pp. 136–137.

8. Gertrude Farber, *Der Mythos "Inanna und Enki" unter besondere Berücksichtigung der Liste der Me,* Studia Pohl, vol. 10 (Rome: Biblical Institute Press, 1973).

9. Samuel Noah Kramer, *Sumerian Mythology,* rev. ed. (Philadelphia: University of Pennsylvania Press, 1972), pp. 65, 64.

10. Stanley Mayer Burstein, *The Babyloniaca of Berossus,* Sources from the Ancient Near East, vol. 1, no. 5 (Malibu, Calif.: Undena Publications, 1978), pp. 1–14.

11. S. H. Hooke, *Babylonian and Assyrian Religion* (London: Hutchinson, 1953), p. 18.

12. Dietz O. Edzard, "Nabu," in Hans W. Haussig, *Wörterbuch der Mythologie,* vol. 1. (Stuttgart: Ernst Klett Verlag, 1965), pp. 106–107.

13. Exodus 31:18.

14. Thomas Astle, *The Origin and Progress of Writing*, 2d ed. (London: J. White, 1803), p. 12, argued that writing existed prior to the Tables of the Law because Exodus 17:14 already referred to "writing in a book." According to Ernst Doblhofer, *Voices in Stone* (New York: Viking Press, 1961), p. 14, some considered the text of the Tables of the Law in Exodus 31:18 as "divine writing," compared to "human writing" noted in Isaiah 8:1.

15. Daniel Defoe, *An Essay upon Literature* (London: Thomas Bowles, 1726), title page.

16. Madeleine V.-David, *Le Débat sur les écritures et l'hiéroglyphe aux XVII et XVIIIe siècles* (Paris: Bibliothèque Générale de l'École Pratique des Hautes Études VIe Section, SEVPEN, 1965), p. 13.

17. John Wilkins, *Essay towards a Real Character and a Philosophical Language* (London: Gellibrand, 1668), p. 11.

18. William Warburton, *Divine Legation of Moses* (London: Fletcher Gyles, 1738), bk. 4, pp. 67, 70–71, 81, 139.

19. Abbé Etienne Mallet, "Ecriture," in Denis Diderot and Jean Le Rond d'Alembert, *Encyclopédie*, vol. 5 (Paris: Briasson, David, Le Breton, Durand, 1755), pp. 358–359.

20. Gelb, *A Study of Writing*, p. 62.

21. George A. Barton, *The Origin and Development of Babylonian Writing* (Baltimore: Johns Hopkins University Press, 1913), p. xiv.

22. William A. Mason, *A History of the Art of Writing* (New York: Macmillan, 1928), pp. 236–237.

23. ATU 25, 52.

24. Edward Chiera, *They Wrote on Clay* (Chicago: University of Chicago Press, 1938), pp. 50, 58–60; Georges Roux, *Ancient Iraq* (Harmondsworth: Penguin Books, 1980), p. 80.

25. "Les linguistes qui se sont attachés à l'étude de l'origine de l'écriture ont souvent considéré les pictographies en projetant sur elles une mentalité née de la pratique de l'écriture. . . . [A]ussi parait-il impossible de se servir de la pictographie des Esquimaux ou des Indiens comme d'un terme de comparaison pour comprendre l'idéographie des peuples antérieurs à l'écriture." André Leroi-Gourhan, *Le Geste et la parole*, vol. 1, (Paris: Editions Albin Michel, 1964), pp. 269–270.

26. V. Gordon Childe, *What Happened in History*, rev. ed. (Harmondsworth: Penguin Books, 1954), p. 93.

27. Chiera, *They Wrote on Clay*, p. 51.

28. Robert Claiborne, *The Birth of Writing* (Alexandria, Va.: Time-Life Books, 1974), p. 66; Dora Jane Hamblin, *The First Cities* (New York: Time-Life Books, 1973), p. 99.

29. Childe, *What Happened*, p. 87; Samuel A. B. Mercer, *The Origin of Writing and Our Alphabet* (London: Luzac and Company, 1959), p. 1.

30. Seton Lloyd, *The Archaeology of Mesopotamia* (London: Thames and Hudson, 1978), p. 55.

31. David Diringer, *The Alphabet,* vol. 1, 3d ed. (London: Hutchinson, 1968), pp. 24, 49.

32. Carleton S. Coon, *Cave Explorations in Iran,* University Museum Monographs (Philadelphia: University of Pennsylvania, 1949), p. 75.

33. Vivian L. Broman, "Jarmo Figurines," master's thesis, Radcliffe College, Cambridge, Mass., 1958. The work was later published as "Jarmo Figurines and Other Clay Objects," in Linda S. Braidwood et al., eds., *Prehistoric Archaeology along the Zagros Flanks,* Oriental Institute Publications 105 (Chicago: University of Chicago Press, 1983), pp. 369–423.

34. Broman, "Jarmo Figurines" (1958), pp. 58, 62, 63; Thorkild Jacobsen, *Human Origins, Selected Readings,* ser. 2, 2d ed. (Chicago: University of Chicago Press, 1946), p. 245.

35. A. Leo Oppenheim, "On an Operational Device in Mesopotamian Bureaucracy," *Journal of Near Eastern Studies* 18 (1959): 121–128.

36. Richard F. S. Starr, *Nuzi,* vol. 1 (Cambridge: Harvard University Press, 1939), pp. 316–317; Ernest R. Lacheman, *Excavations at Nuzi,* vol. 7, Economic and Social Documents, Harvard Semitic Series, vol. 16 (Cambridge: Harvard University Press, 1958), p. 88, no. 311.

37. It is likely that the normal tablet was meant for Puhisenni's archive and the egg-shaped envelope was intended for the shepherd Ziqarru, who was probably illiterate: Starr, *Nuzi,* pp. 316–317; Lacheman, *Excavations at Nuzi,* p. v. Tzvi Abusch explains why both texts were found in the same archive in "Notes on a Pair of Matching Texts: A Shepherd's Bulla and an Owner's Receipt," in Martha A. Morrison and David I. Owen, eds., *Studies on the Civilization and Culture of Nuzi and the Hurrians* (Winona Lake, Ind.: Eisenbrauns, 1981), pp. 1–9.

38. Abusch, "Notes," pp. 2–3.

39. Starr, *Nuzi,* p. 316.

40. Oppenheim, "On an Operational Device," pp. 125–126.

41. The Sumerian form is borrowed into Akkadian as *tuk(k)annu* (personal communication, Marcel Sigrist). The text is published in G. Pettinato, S. A. Picchioni, and F. Reshid, *Testi Economici Dell'Iraq Museum-Baghdad,* Materiali per il Vocabulario Neosumerico, vol. 8, (Rome: Multigrafica Editrice, 1979), pl. XLVIII, no. 148; P. Dhorme, "Tablettes de Drehem à Jérusalem," *Revue d'Assyriologie et d'Archéologie Orientale* 9 (1912): pl. I: SA 19.

42. Starr, *Nuzi,* p. 316.

43. Pierre Amiet, "Il y a 5000 ans les Elamites inventaient l'écriture," *Archeologia* 12 (1966): 20–22.

44. "On peut ainsi se demander si [le scribe] ne s'inspirait pas des petits objets de terre enfermés dans les bulles, et qui symboliseraient très conventionnellement certaines denrées." Ibid., p. 22.

45. Amiet assumed that Nineveh also yielded an envelope, but the artifact he had in mind is a solid oval bulla. Pierre Amiet, *Elam* (Auvers-sur-Oise: Archée Editeur, 1966), p. 70.

46. "Une série d'encoches rondes ou allongées, semblable aux chiffres que l'on observe sur les tablettes, et qui correspondent au nombre que donne l'addition des calculi serrés à l'intérieur, à cela près que leurs formes ne sont pas aussi diversifiées que celles des derniers." M 43, p. 69.

47. "Je me demandais donc si cette écriture ne s'inspirait pas de certains des calculi enfermés dans les bulles." Pierre Amiet, *L'Age des échanges inter-iraniens* (Paris: Editions de la Réunion des Musées Nationaux, 1986), p. 76.

48. "L'écriture a copié, ici comme ailleurs, ce qui existait en vrai." Maurice Lambert, "Pourquoi l'écriture est née en Mésopotamie," *Archeologia* 12 (1966): 30.

49. Denise Schmandt-Besserat: "The Use of Clay before Pottery in the Zagros," *Expedition* 16, no. 2, (1974): 10−17; "An Archaic Recording System and the Origin of Writing," *Syro-Mesopotamian Studies* 1, no. 2 (1977): 1−32; "The Earliest Precursor of Writing," *Scientific American* 238, no. 6 (1978): 50−58.

50. Denise Schmandt-Besserat: "Tokens and Counting," *Biblical Archaeologist* 46 (1983): 117−120; "Before Numerals," *Visible Language* 18, no. 1 (1986): 48−60.

1. WHAT ARE TOKENS?

1. "Une activité particulièrement importante à Tell Aswad, surtout dans le niveau II au cours de la première moitié du 7ᵉ millénaire, était la fabrication de petits objets en argile modelée et durcie au feu. . . . Il s'agit . . . d'objets de formes géometriques, telles que boules, disques et coupelles." Henri de Contenson, "Recherches sur le Néolithique de Syrie (1967−76)," *Comptes Rendus, Académie des Inscriptions et Belles-Lettres* (1979): 821−822.

2. Cyril S. Smith, "A Matter of Form," *Isis* 76, no. 4 (1985): 586.

3. This and the following such parenthetical references correspond to the types and subtypes illustrated in Part Three of this book.

4. Sabah Aboud Jasim, *The Ubaid Period in Iraq*, pt. 1, International Series 267 (Oxford: BAR, 1985), pp. 69−73.

5. Seton Lloyd and Fuad Safar, "Tell Hassuna: Excavations by the Iraq Government Directorate General of Antiquities in 1943 and 1944," *Journal of Near Eastern Studies* 4 (1945): 258.

6. Ernest Mackay, *Report on Excavations at Jemdet Nasr, Iraq*, Anthropology Memoirs, vol. 1, no. 3 (Chicago: Field Museum of Natural History, 1931), p. 278.

7. M. E. L. Mallowan and J. Cruikshank Rose, "Excavations at Tell Arpachiyah, 1933," *Iraq* 2, pt. 1 (1935): 88.

8. Lloyd and Safar, "Tell Hassuna," pl. X, 1: 22−23.

9. Arthur J. Tobler, *Excavations at Tepe Gawra*, vol. 2, University Museum Monographs (Philadelphia: University of Pennsylvania, 1950), pp. 170−171, 205.

10. H. R. Hall, *Ur Excavations,* vol. 1, *Al Ubaid* (Oxford: Oxford University Press, 1927), p. 41, fig. 4.

11. Vivian L. Broman, "Jarmo Figurines," master's thesis, Radcliffe College, Cambridge, Mass., 1958. The work was later published as "Jarmo Figurines and Other Clay Objects," in Linda S. Braidwood et al., eds., *Prehistoric Archaeology along the Zagros Flanks,* Oriental Institute Publications 105 (Chicago: University of Chicago Press, 1983), pp. 369–423.

2. WHERE TOKENS WERE HANDLED AND WHO USED THEM

1. Georges Charbonnier, *Conversations with Claude Lévi-Strauss* (London: Jonathan Cape, 1961), pp. 29–30.

2. Robert J. Braidwood, Bruce Howe, and Charles A. Reed, "The Iranian Prehistoric Project," *Science* 133, no. 3469 (1961): 2008; Philip E. L. Smith, "Ganj Dareh Tepe," *Paléorient* 2, no. 1 (1974): 207; Philip E. L. Smith, "An Interim Report on Ganj Dareh Tepe, Iran," *American Journal of Archaeology* 82, no. 4 (1978): 538.

3. Henri de Contenson: "Chronologie absolue de Tell Aswad (Damascène, Syrie)," *Bulletin de la Société Préhistorique Française* 70 (1973): 253; "Tell Aswad (Damascène)," *Paléorient* 5 (1979): 155; "La Région de Damas au Néolithique," *Annales Archéologiques Arabes Syriennes* 35 (1985): 9. Jacques Cauvin, *Les Premiers Villages de Syrie-Palestine du IXème au VIIème millénaire avant J. C.,* Collection de la Maison de L'Orient Mediterranéen Ancien, no. 4, Série Archéologique 3 (Lyons: Maison de l'Orient, 1978), p. 136.

4. Carleton S. Coon, *Cave Explorations in Iran,* University Museum Monographs (Philadelphia: University of Pennsylvania, 1949), p. 75; Frank Hole, "Tepe Tula'i: An Early Campsite in Khuzistan, Iran," *Paléorient* 2 (1974): fig. 15h, o–t.

5. Personal communication, Henri de Contenson.

6. Henry T. Wright, Naomi Miller, and Richard Redding, "Time and Process in an Uruk Rural Center," in *L'Archéologie de l'Iraq du début de l'époque néolithique à 333 avant notre ère* (Paris: Colloques Internationaux du Centre National de la Recherche Scientifique, 1980), p. 277.

7. UVB 17, pp. 36–37, pl. 24g–h, m–n, p–t, and v.

8. UVB 17, p. 37; UVB 22, p. 40.

9. Yvonne Rosengarten, *Le Concept sumérien de consommation dans la vie économique et religieuse.* (Paris: Editions E. de Boccard, 1960), p. 32.

10. Personal communication, Frank Hole.

11. Cat. no. 43, 71–129, BW; T. Cuyler Young, Jr., and Louis D. Levine, *Excavations of the Godin Project: Second Progress Report,* Art and Archaeology Occasional Paper 26 (Toronto: Royal Ontario Museum, 1974), p. 61, fig. 6: G 20.

12. Cat. nos. 21: 71–144 and 51: 71–143, BW; Young and Levine, *Excavations of the Godin Project,* p. 59, fig. 4.

13. Ghanim Wahida, "The Excavations of the Third Season at Tell as-Sawwan, 1966," *Sumer* 23, nos. 1–2 (1967): 169.

14. Mary M. Voigt, *Hajji Firuz Tepe, Iran: The Neolithic Settlement,* Hasanlu Excavations Reports, vol. 1, University Museum Monograph no. 50 (Philadelphia: University of Pennsylvania, 1983), p. 182, HF 68–81.

15. Martha Prickett, "Man, Land and Water: Settlement Distribution and the Development of Irrigation Agriculture in the Upper Rud-i Gushk Drainage, Southeastern Iran," Ph.D dissertation, Harvard University, 1985, p. 539.

16. Personal communication, Philip E. L. Smith.

17. Voigt, *Hajji Firuz Tepe,* pp. 87, 181–184, H.F. 68–122, 68–170–172, 68–189, and 68–195.

18. Ibid., pp. 47–49.

19. Sabah Aboud Jasim and Joan Oates, "Early Tokens and Tablets in Mesopotamia: New Information from Tell Abada and Tell Brak," *World Archaeology* 17, no. 3 (1986): 352–355.

20. UVB 25, p. 40.

21. M 29, pp. 13, 17–18, 25, 27, and fig. 23.

22. Prickett, "Man, Land and Water," p. 539.

23. Jasim and Oates, "Early Tokens," pp. 352, 355.

24. Ibid., p. 355.

25. I am thankful to Marcel Sigrist for communicating to me the following two references: D. Calvot, *Textes économiques de Selluš-Dagan du Musée du Louvre et du Collège de France,* Materiali per il Vocabulario Neo-sumerico, vol. 8 (Rome: Multigrafica Editrice, 1979), pl. XLVIII, MVN 8, 147; P. Dhorme, "Tablettes de Drehem à Jérusalem," *Revue d'Assyriologie et d'Archéologie Orientale* 9 (1912): pl. I: SA 19.

26. Cauvin, *Les Premiers Villages,* pp. 74, 73, 43.

27. Olivier Aurenche et al., "Chronologie et organisation de l'espace dans le Proche Orient," *Préhistoire du Levant,* Colloque CNRS no. 598 (Lyons, 1980), pp. 7–8.

28. Rainer Protsch and Rainer Berger, "Earliest Radiocarbon Dates for Domesticated Animals," *Science* 179, no. 4070 (1973): 237; Sandor Bökönyi, Robert J. Braidwood, and Charles A. Reed, "Earliest Animal Domestication Dated?" *Science* 182 (1973): 1161.

29. Henri de Genouillac, *Fouilles de Telloh,* vol. 1, *Epoques présargoniques* (Paris: Paul Geuthner, 1934), p. 64; M 46, p. 151 and pl. 89; P. P. Delougaz and Helene J. Kantor, "New Evidence for the Prehistoric and Protoliterate Culture Development of Khuzestan," *The Memorial Volume of the Vth International Congress of Iranian Art and Archaeology,* vol. 1 (Tehran, 1972), p. 27; André Finet, "Bilan provisoire des fouilles belges du Tell Kannas," *Annual of the American Schools of Oriental Research* 44 (1979): 93.

30. Eva Strommenger, "The Chronological Division of the Archaic Levels of Uruk-Eanna VI to III/II: Past and Present," *American Journal of Archaeology* 84, no. 4 (1980): 485–486; Louis Le Breton, "The Early Pe-

riods at Susa, Mesopotamian Relations," *Iraq* 19, no. 2 (1957): 97–113; Delougaz and Kantor, "New Evidence," pp. 26–33.

31. Hans J. Nissen, *Grundzüge einer Geschichte der Frühzeit des vorderen Orients* (Darmstadt: Wissenschaftliche Buchgesellschaft, 1983), pp. 92–93.

32. M 43, pl. 18: 695; Delougaz and Kantor, "New Evidence," p. 32, pl. Xc. The En is represented on an oblong bulla from Habuba Kabira: 72 Hb 102 (personal communication, Eva Strommenger).

33. UVB 3, pls. 10 and 13.

34. Faisal El-Wailly and Behnam Abu Es-Soof, "Excavations at Tell es-Sawwan, First Preliminary Report (1964)," *Sumer* 21, nos. 1–2 (1965): 26, 28; M. E. L. Mallowan and J. Cruikshank Rose, "Excavations at Tell Arpachiyah, 1933," *Iraq* 2, pt. 1 (1935): 40; Arthur J. Tobler, *Excavations at Tepe Gawra,* vol. 2, University Museum Monographs (Philadelphia: University of Pennsylvania, 1950), Grave 181 (pp. 117–118, 205, pls. XCVI.a: 2, 3, 5, 7–12 and CLXXIX: 53), Locus 7–58 (pp. 116, 120, 170 and pl. LXXXIV.c.), Tombs 102, 107, 110, and 114 (pp. 84–85, 94–96, pls. XXII, XXVII, and XLVI.a).

35. Peder Mortensen, "Additional Remarks on the Chronology of Early Village-Farming Communities in the Zagros Area," *Sumer* 20 (1964): 28–36; Voigt, *Hajji Firuz Tepe,* p. 87, HF 68–122, 170, 171, 189, 195.

36. Voigt, *Hajji Firuz Tepe,* pp. 86–87, H12 B3.

37. El-Wailly and Abu Es-Soof, "Excavations," p. 23; Mallowan and Cruikshank Rose, "Excavations," p. 35; Tobler, *Excavations,* pp. 106–107.

38. Tobler, *Excavations,* pp. 70–75, pls. XXIV and XLVI.a.

39. Voigt, *Hajji Firuz Tepe,* p. 254.

40. El-Wailly and Abu Es-Soof, "Excavations," pp. 26, 28.

41. Tobler, *Excavations,* p. 199, pl. CLXXV, and figs. 74-76.

42. Ibid., pp. 94–96, pls. LIII.b, c, e; LV.a: 1 and 4; LVIII.a: 1 and b: 3; LIX.a: 6–8; CIII: 7–8; CIV: 13–14, 20–21; CVI: 37–38; CVII: 55–56; CVIII: 58, 60, and 65.

43. Voigt, *Hajji Firuz Tepe,* pp. 146–151, Structure VI.

44. Tobler, *Excavations,* pp. 110–111.

45. Ibid.

46. El-Wailly and Abu Es-Soof, "Excavations," pp. 28, 26.

47. Tobler, *Excavations,* pp. 84–85, 116.

48. Ibid., pp. 84–85.

49. Ibid., p. 94.

50. Ibid., pp. 84, 96.

51. Ibid., pp. 84–85.

52. El-Wailly and Abu Es-Soof, "Excavations," p. 28.

3. STRINGS OF TOKENS AND ENVELOPES

1. "En secouant . . . [les boules de terre crue] . . . près de l'oreille, on entend le bruit de petits objects s'entrechoquant dans la cavité intérieure;

plusieurs d'entre elles ayant été rompues dans le dégagement, nous avons reconnu la présence de petites masses d'argile cuite aux formes variées: grains, cones, pyramides, pastilles de 1 cm. de diamètre." R. de Mecquenem, "Fouilles de Suse," *Revue d'Assyriologie et d'Archéologie Orientale* 21, no. 3 (1924): 106.

2. M 43, p. 70.

3. M 43, 510, 540, 541, 544, 547, 567, 585, 599, 644, 649, 665; Dafi 8a, pp. 20–21, pl. V; Dafi 9b, p. 72.

4. P. P. Delougaz and Helene J. Kantor, "New Evidence for the Prehistoric and Protoliterate Culture Development of Khuzestan," *The Memorial Volume of the Vth International Congress of Iranian Art and Archaeology,* vol. 1 (Tehran, 1972), p. 27.

5. Eva Strommenger, *Habuba Kabira* (Mainz am Rhein: Verlag Philipp von Zabern, 1980), p. 63 and fig. 57.

6. At Susa, a perforated token and a bulla were located in the same square, J-4, room 830: Dafi 9b, p. 142, fig. 40: 9, and p. 64.

7. Dafi 8a, p. 35.

8. In Susa: Sb 1945 bis and 4850. In Habuba Kabira: Eva Strommenger, "Habuba Kabira am syrischen Euphrat," *Antike Welt* 8, no. 1 (1977): 19, fig. 13b.

9. I am thankful to W. David Kingery, head of the Ceramics Department, MIT, for the analyses.

10. M 43, pp. 69–70; Dafi 8a, pp. 15–18.

11. Delougaz and Kantor, "New Evidence," p. 27.

12. Henry T. Wright, *An Early Town in the Deh Luran Plain,* Memoirs of the Museum of Anthropology, no. 13 (Ann Arbor: University of Michigan, 1981), p. 156; Denise Schmandt-Besserat and S. M. Alexander, *The First Civilization: The Legacy of Sumer* (Austin, Texas: University Museum, 1975), pp. 51, 53; Ali Hakemi, *Catalogue de l'exposition: Lut Shahdad "Xabis"* (Tehran, 1972), p. 20, item 54 and pl. 22A.

13. UVB 21, pp. 30–32 and pls. 17–19.

14. Dietrich Sürenhagen and E. Töpperwein, "Kleinen Funde," Vierter vorläufiger Bericht über die von der deutschen Orientgesellschaft mit Mitteln der Stiftung Volkswagenwerk in Habuba Kabira und Mumbaqat unternommenen archäologischen Untersuchungen, *Mitteilungen der deutschen Orientgesellschaft,* vol. 105 (1973), pp. 21, 26; Denise Schmandt-Besserat, "Tokens, Envelopes and Impressed Tablets at Habuba Kabira," in Eva Strommenger and Kay Kohlmeyer, eds., *Habuba Kabira Süd — Die kleinen Funde,* Wissenschaftliche Veröffentlichung der deutschen Orientgesellschaft (forthcoming); Johannes Boese, "Excavations at Tell Sheikh Hassan, Preliminary Report on the 1987 Campaign in the Euphrates Valley," *Annales Archéologiques Arabes Syriennes* 36–37 (1986–1987): 77, fig. 36a, b.

15. Stephen Reimer, "Tell Qraya," *Syrian Archaeology Bulletin* 1 (1988): 6.

16. Collection of Shucri Sahuri, Amman, Jordan.

17. Collection of Thomas C. Barger, La Jolla, Calif.

18. Wright, *An Early Town,* p. 156.

19. Delougaz and Kantor, "New Evidence," p. 27; Helene J. Kantor and P. P. Delougaz, "New Light on the Emergence of Civilization in the Near East," *Unesco Courier* (November 1969): 23.

20. Personal communication, C. C. Lamberg-Karlovsky.

21. Eva Strommenger, "The Chronological Division of the Archaic Levels of Uruk-Eanna VI to III/II: Past and Present," *American Journal of Archaeology* 84, no. 4 (1980): 485–486; Dietrich Sürenhagen, "Archaische Keramik aus Uruk-Warka. Erster Teil: Die Keramik der Schichten XVI–VI aus den Sondagen 'Tiefschnitt' und 'Sägegraben' in Eanna," BaM 17 (1986): 7–95.

22. Dafi 8a, p. 31.

23. Dafi 8b, pp. 62, 78.

24. Reinhard Dittmann, *Betrachtungen zur Frühzeit des Südwest-Iran,* pt. 1 (Berlin: Dietrich Reimer Verlag, 1986), p. 102.

25. Dafi 8b, pp. 76, 62.

26. UVB 15, p. 21, W 18987; UVB 17, p. 26.

27. M 29, pp. 17, 18.

28. Dafi 8a, p. 36; Dafi 9a, p. 14, fig. 1.

29. Personal communication, C. C. Lamberg-Karlovsky.

30. Sb 1927, 1936, 1940, and 4338.

31. Susa: Sb 1930, 1938, 1942, 1967, 5340, 6350, 6946, no reference; S.ACR.I.77: 1999.1, 2049.1, 2067.2, 2089.1, 2111.2, 2111.3, 2130.1, 2130.4, 2142.2, 2142.3, 2173.4. Chogha Mish: Delougaz and Kantor, "New Evidence," p. 27, pl. IXa. Uruk: W 20987.3; W 20987.7; W 20987.8; W 20987.15; W 20987.17. Habuba Kabira: MII: 133, MII: 134.

32. Wright, *An Early Town,* p. 156.

33. UVB 21, p. 32 and pl. 19b, W 20987.27.

34. Delougaz and Kantor, "New Evidence," p. 30, pl. IXb.

35. The first group is stored at the Louvre: Dafi 8a, p. 18, S.ACR.I.77.2091.2 and S.ACR.I.77.2067.3.

36. Delougaz and Kantor, "New Evidence," p. 27.

37. Pierre Amiet, *L'Age des échanges inter-iraniens,* Notes et Documents des Musées de France, vol. 11 (Paris: Ministère de la Culture et de la Communication, Editions de la Réunion des Musées Nationaux, 1986), p. 85 and pls. 29, 31: 7, 8.

38. Sb 5340.

39. Sb 1927, 1940, 2286, 6350; S.ACR.I.77.2089.1, 2111.3, 2130.1, 2130.2, 2142.2, 2142.3, 2162.1, 2173.4.

40. Sb 1927.

41. Sb 1927.

42. Dafi 8a, fig. 3: 3.

43. MII: 133.

44. Sb 1940.

45. Sb 1932.

46. Sb 1928, 1929, 1936, 1944, 1950, 1974, and 1978.

47. Mona Spangler Phillips, "The Manufacture of Ancient Middle Eastern Clay Envelopes," *Technology and Culture* 24, no. 2 (1983): 256–257.

48. Sb 1936.

4. IMPRESSED TABLETS

1. Georges Charbonnier, *Conversations with Claude Lévi-Strauss* (London: Cape Editions, 1973), p. 30.

2. M 17, p. 1; M 43, pp. 68–69; Dafi 1c, p. 236, fig. 43; Dafi 3, pp. 93–94, fig. 14; Dafi 8a, pp. 18–20, pl. IV, fig. 4.

3. Harvey Weiss and T. Cuyler Young, Jr., "The Merchants of Susa: Godin V and the Plateau Lowlands Relations in the Late Fourth Millennium B.C.," *Iran* 13 (1975): 8–11.

4. Roman Ghirshman, *Fouilles de Sialk,* vol. 1 (Paris: Paul Geuthner, 1938), pp. 65–68, pls. XCII–XCIII.

5. Donald S. Whitcomb, "The Proto-Elamite Period at Tall-i Ghazir, Iran," master's thesis, University of Georgia, Athens, 1971, p. 31, pl. XIA.

6. P. P. Delougaz and Helene J. Kantor, "The Iranian Expedition: Chogha Mish Excavations," in *The Oriental Institute Report for 1967–68* (Chicago: Oriental Institute, University of Chicago), p. 11; Helene J. Kantor, "Excavations at Chogha Mish," *The Oriental Institute Report for 1974–75* (Chicago: Oriental Institute, University of Chicago), p. 22; Helene J. Kantor, "Excavations at Chogha Mish: 1974–75," *Second Annual Report* (Los Angeles: Institute of Archaeology, University of California), pp. 10, 17: 6–7.

7. UVB 3, p. 29, pl. 19b; UVB 4, p. 28, pl. 14c–h (W 9656 h, ea; W 9656 eb); UVB 5, p. 14, pl. 14b, d (W 14148, 14210); UVB 8, p. 51, pl. 51c (W 16184); UVB 17, p. 56 (W 19727); Adam Falkenstein, "Zu den Inschriften der Grabung in Uruk-Warka, 1960–61," BaM 2 (1963): 2 (W 20239); UVB 20, p. 23, pl. 26g, 28c (W 20777); UVB 22, pp. 59–60, nos. 134–140 (W 21300-1–7); UVB 23, pp. 37–38 (W 21452), p. 40 (W 21654.1); UVB 25, p. 38, pl. 27k, n (W 21859); ZATU 34.

8. Henri Frankfort, "Progress of the Work of the Oriental Institute in Iraq, 1934–35: Fifth Preliminary Report of the Iraq Expedition," OIC no. 20 (1936): 25, fig. 19.

9. Dominique Collon and Julian Reade, "Archaic Nineveh," BaM 14 (1983): 33.

10. Dietrich Sürenhagen and E. Töpperwein, "Kleinen Funde," Vierter vorläufiger Bericht über die von der deutschen Orientgesellschaft mit Mitteln der Stiftung Volkswagenwerk in Habuba Kabira und Mumbaqat unternommenen archäologischen Untersuchungen, *Mitteilungen der deutschen Orientgesellschaft,* vol. 105 (1973), pp. 20–21, fig. 4; Eva Strommenger, "Ausgrabungen in Habuba Kabira und Mumbaqat," *Archiv für Orientforschung* 24 (1973): 170–171, fig. 17; Eva Strommenger, "Habuba Kabira am syrischen Euphrat," *Antike Welt* 8, no. 1 (1977): 18, fig. 11; Eva Strommen-

ger, "Ausgrabungen der deutschen Orient-Gesellschaft in Habuba Kabira," in David Noel Freedman, ed., *Archeological Reports from the Tabqa Dam Project—Euphrates Valley, Syria* (Cambridge, Mass.: American Schools of Oriental Research, 1979), p. 68, fig. 14.

11. G. van Driel, "Tablets from Jebel Aruda," in G. van Driel, Th. J. H. Krispijn, M. Stol, and K. R. Veenhof, eds., *Zikir Šumim,* Assyriological Studies Presented to F. R. Kraus on the Occasion of His Seventieth Birthday (Leiden: E. J. Brill, 1982), p. 12.

12. John Curtis, ed., *Fifty Years of Mesopotamian Discovery* (London: British School of Archaeology in Iraq, 1982), pp. 64–65, fig. 51.

13. André Parrot, "Les Fouilles de Mari, quatorzième campagne (printemps 1964)," *Syria* 42 (1965): 12.

14. Dafi 8a, p. 19.

15. Denise Schmandt-Besserat, "Tokens, Envelopes and Impressed Tablets at Habuba Kabira," in Eva Strommenger and Kay Kohlmeyer, eds., *Habuba Kabira Süd—Die kleinen Funde,* Wissenschaftliche Veröffentlichung der deutschen Orientgesellschaft (forthcoming).

16. UVB 3, p. 29.

17. Weiss and Young, "Merchants of Susa," p. 3.

18. ZATU 48–49.

19. Weiss and Young, "Merchants of Susa," p. 8.

20. G. van Driel and C. van Driel-Murray, "Jebel Aruda 1977–1978," *Akkadica* 12 (1979): 24.

21. Collon and Reade, "Archaic Nineveh," p. 33.

22. "Sur le sol, par dessous les éboulis du toit de la longue pièce en T du temple C, au niveau IVa." UVB 22, pp. 59–60, nos. 134–140 (W 21300–1–7).

23. ZATU 39–40.

24. Weiss and Young, "Merchants of Susa," p. 9, fig. 4: 2.

25. Ghirshman, *Fouilles de Sialk,* pls. XCII–XCIII.

26. UVB 3, p. 29; ZATU 48.

27. Gd 73–64 and 286, Weiss and Young, "Merchants of Susa," p. 9, fig. 4: 5 and 6.

28. Ibid., fig. 4: 6.

29. Ibid., fig. 4: 5.

30. Gd 73–292, ibid., p. 10, fig. 5: 1.

31. Ibid.

32. ZATU.

33. Hans J. Nissen, Peter Damerow, and Robert K. Englund, *Archaic Bookkeeping* (Chicago: University of Chicago Press, 1990).

34 ATU.

35. Jöran Friberg, *The Third Millennium Roots of Babylonian Mathematics. I. A Method for the Decipherment, through Mathematical and Metrological Analysis, of Proto-Sumerian and Proto-Elamite Semi-pictographic Inscriptions* (Göteborg: Chalmers University of Technology and University of Göteborg, 1978–1979).

36. A. A. Vaiman: "Über die Protosumerische Schrift," *Acta Antiqua Academiae Scientiarum Hungaricae* 22 (1974): 17–22; "Protosumerische Mass- und Zählsysteme," BaM 20 (1989): 114–120.

37. P. P. Delougaz and Helene J. Kantor, "New Evidence for the Prehistoric and Protoliterate Culture Development of Khuzestan," *The Memorial Volume of the Vth International Congress of Iranian Art and Archaeology,* vol. 1 (Tehran, 1972), p. 30, pl. IXb.

38. Sb 1938, M 43, p. 95: 582, pl. 72.

39. Denise Schmandt-Besserat and S. M. Alexander, *The First Civilization: The Legacy of Sumer* (Austin, Texas: University Museum, 1975), pp. 51, 53.

40. Sb 6350, M 43, p. 66, pl. 61: 460 bis; Sb 1927, M 43, p. 91, pl. 68: 539.

41. Kantor, "Excavations: 1974–75," p. 17, fig. 6.

42. Gd 73–64, obverse, Weiss and Young, "Merchants of Susa," p. 9, fig 4: 5.

43. Driel, "Tablets," p. 14: 1, 2, 4.

44. Frankfort, "Progress," p. 25.

45. Ghirshman, *Fouilles de Sialk,* p. 67, pl. XCIII: S 539.

46. Sb 4839, M 43, p. 100: 629.

47. W 9656 eb, UVB 4, p. 28, pl. 14.

48. Peter Damerow and Robert K. Englund, "Die Zahlzeichensysteme der archaischen Texte aus Uruk," ZATU 136; Friberg, *Third Millennium Roots,* p. 10; Vaiman, "Protosumerische Schrift," p. 19.

49. Sb 1927, M 43, p. 91: 539, pl. 68.

50. Sb 6959, M 43, p. 101: 642, pl. 79.

51. Delougaz and Kantor, "New Evidence," p. 30, pl. IXb.

52. Sb 1927, M 43, p. 91: 539, pl. 68.

53. Driel, "Tablets," p. 14: 1 and 6.

54. Sb 2313, M 43, p. 128: 622; MT, M 43, p. 91: 545, pl. 68.

55. Nissen, Damerow, and Englund, *Archaic Bookkeeping,* p. 29; Friberg, *Third Millennium Roots,* p. 10.

56. S.ACR.I.77.2173.4, Dafi 8a, p. 15, no. 2, pl. I: 3, fig. 3: 3.

57. Nissen, Damerow, and Englund, *Archaic Bookkeeping,* p. 29; Vaiman, "Protosumerische Schrift," p. 19.

58. Nissen, Damerow, and Englund, *Archaic Bookkeeping,* p. 57; Friberg, *Third Millennium Roots,* p. 46.

59. Gd 73–299, unpublished.

60. ATU 918.

61. Friberg, *Third Millennium Roots,* p. 46.

62. Gd 73–291, unpublished.

63. Vaiman, "Protosumerische Schrift," p. 19; Friberg, *Third Millennium Roots,* p. 25.

64. Delougaz and Kantor, "New Evidence," p. 30, pl. IXb.

65. Sb 1967, M. 43, p. 86, pl. 64: 488.

66. W 20987.15, unpublished.

67. S.ACR.I.77.2173.4, Dafi 8a, p. 15, no. 2; pl. I: 3, fig. 3: 3.

68. Schmandt-Besserat and Alexander, *The First Civilization,* pp. 51 and 53.

69. Weiss and Young, "Merchants of Susa," p. 9, fig. 4: 1–6 and fig. 5: 1.

70. Driel, "Tablets," p. 14: 1–4 and pp. 15, 7, 13.

71. MII: 128, unpublished.

72. Frankfort, "Progress," p. 25.

73. Collon and Reade, "Archaic Nineveh," p. 34, fig. 1a.

74. Ghirshman, *Fouilles de Sialk,* pl. XCIII, S 539.

75. Sb 2312, M 43, p. 87, pl. 65: 491; Sb 2316, M 43, p. 85, pl. 63: 475; Sb 6289, M 43, p. 102, pl. 67: 650.

76. W 10133 a and b, UVB 3, p. 29, pl. 19b.

77. Nissen, Damerow, and Englund, *Archaic Bookkeeping,* p. 29; Friberg, *Third Millennium Roots,* p. 10; Vaiman, "Protosumerische Schrift," p. 19.

78. Sb 1932, Pierre Amiet, *L'Age des échanges inter-iraniens* (Paris: Ministère de la Culture et de la Communication, 1986), p. 85, fig. 29.

79. Delougaz and Kantor, "New Evidence," p. 30, pl. IXb.

80. Sb 1967, M 43, p. 86, pl. 64: 488.

81. Sb 2315, M 43, p. 89: 521, pl. 66.

82. MII: 128 and 130, unpublished.

83. Driel, "Tablets," p. 14, fig. 3.

84. Nissen, Damerow, and Englund, *Archaic Bookkeeping,* p. 29; Friberg, *Third Millennium Roots,* p. 10; Vaiman, "Protosumerische Schrift," p. 19.

85. MII: 130, unpublished; MII: 128, Strommenger, "Ausgrabungen in Habuba Kabira und Mumbaqat," p. 171, fig. 17.

86. Weiss and Young, "Merchants of Susa," p. 9, fig. 4: 5, Gd 73–64.

87. Ghirshman, *Fouilles de Sialk,* pl. XCIII, S 1627.

88. Sb 1966 bis, M 43, p. 104: 671, pl. 82; Sb 1975 bis, M 43, p. 101: 641, pl. 79.

89. Nissen, Damerow, and Englund, *Archaic Bookkeeping,* p.29; Vaiman, "Protosumerische Shrift," p. 21.

90. Friberg, *Third Millennium Roots,* p. 46.

91. Whitcomb, "Proto-Elamite Period," p. 31, pl. XI.

92. Nissen, Damerow, and Englund, *Archaic Bookkeeping,* p. 57; Friberg, *Third Millennium Roots,* p. 46; Vaiman, "Protosumerische Schrift," fig. 4

93. S.ACR.I.77.2128.2 and 3, Dafi 8a, p. 19, nos. 20 and 23, pl. IV: 7 and 6, fig. 4: 2 and 5.

94. Delougaz and Kantor, "New Evidence," p. 30, pl. IX a and b.

95. Sb 1938, M 43, p. 95, pl. 72: 582.

96. W 20987.8, 15, and 17, unpublished.

97. Sb 6959, M 43, p. 101: 642, pl. 79; Sb 2313, M 43, p. 128: 922, pl. 99.

98. Friberg, *Third Millennium Roots,* p. 10.

99. Sb 1927 and 1940, M 43, p. 91: 539 and p. 92: 555, pl. 68.

100. Susa: Sb 1938 and 1946; S.ACR.2130.4.

101. Chogha Mish: envelope on exhibition at the Oriental Institute, University of Chicago.

102. Sb 2313, M 43, p. 128: 922, pl. 99.

103. S.ACR.I.77.1999.1, Dafi 8a, 1978, p. 17.

104. Sb 1927, M 43, p. 91, pl. 68: 539; Sb 1940, M 43, p. 92, pl. 69: 555.

105. Delougaz and Kantor, "Iranian Expedition," p. 11.

106. Driel, "Tablets," p. 15, fig. 1b: 10.

107. Sb 6299, M 43, p. 104: 666, pl. 81.

108. Curtis, *Fifty Years*, p. 65, fig. 51.

109. W 21859, UVB 25, p. 38, pl. 27k.

110. Friberg, *Third Millennium Roots*, p. 21.

111. Sb 1940, M 43, p. 92: 555.

112. Sb 6299, M 43, p. 104: 666, pl. 81.

113. S.ACR.I.77. 1999.1, Dafi 8a, p. 17; S.ACR.I.77. 2089.1, 2111.2.

114. W 20987.27, UVB 21, pl. 19b.

115. Sb 1940, M 43, p. 92, pl. 69: 555; S.ACR.I.77.2049.1, Dafi 8a, p. 16.

116. Gd 73–293.

117. MII: 127, Eva Strommenger, "Habuba Kabira am syrischen Euphrat," p. 18, fig. 11.

118. Driel, "Tablets," p. 15, fig. 1b: 9 and 10.

119. Sb 4854, M 43, p. 85: 479, pl. 63; Sb 6291, M 43, p. 89: 520, pl. 66; Sb 6299, M 43, p. 104: 666, pl. 81.

120. Curtis, *Fifty Years*, p. 65, fig. 51.

121. W 21859, UVB 25, p. 38, pl. 27k.

122. Friberg, *Third Millennium Roots,* p. 21. The long wedge, standing for one animal, is present in the Uruk archaic tablets (e.g., on W 28859, UVB 25, pl. 27k). This has not been recognized by Nissen, Damerow, and Englund, who have not differentiated between the short and long wedge (*Archaic Bookkeeping*, p. 28).

123. UVB 21, pl. 19b.

124. Kantor, "Excavations: 1974–75," pl. 17: 7.

125. Strommenger, "Ausgrabungen in Habuba Kabira und Mumbaqat," p. 171, fig. 17.

126. Driel, "Tablets," p. 14, fig 1a: 4.

127. W 20987.27, UVB 21, pl. 19b; W 20987.7.

128. MII: 133 and 134; Sürenhagen and Töpperwein, "Kleinen Funde," pp. 21, 26; Schmandt-Besserat, "Tokens, Envelopes and Impressed Tablets at Habuba Kabira."

129. UVB 21, pl. 19b.

130. Delougaz and Kantor, "New Evidence," p. 30, pl. IXb.

131. Gd 73–291, obverse and reverse, unpublished.

132. Nissen, Damerow, and Englund, *Archaic Bookkeeping*, p. 29; Friberg, *Third Millennium Roots*, p. 25; Vaiman, "Protosumerische Schrift," p. 19.

133. Dafi 8a, S.ACR. I.77.2089.1, p. 21, pl. II: 5, fig. 6: 2.

134. Sb 1975 bis, M 43, p. 101, pl. 79: 641.

135. Vaiman, "Protosumerische Schrift," pp. 20–21, fig. 3.

136. Sb 6291, M 43, p. 89: 520, pl. 66.

137. Sb 6289, M 43, p. 90: 534, pl. 67.

138. For example, Sb 4829, M 43, p. 100, pl. 78: 629.

139. For example, Sb 6299, M 43, p. 104, pl. 81: 666.

140. Sb 1966 bis, M 43, p. 104, pl. 82: 671; Sb 1975 bis, M 43, p. 101, pl. 79: 641.

141. Dafi 8a, p. 21, S.ACR.I.77.2073.4.

142. Susa: Sb 1975 bis, M 43, p. 101, pl. 79: 641.

143. UVB 21, pl. 19b; W 20987.7.

144. MII: 134; Schmandt-Besserat, "Tokens, Envelopes and Impressed Tablets at Habuba Kabira."

145. ATU 781 bears an additional incised cross.

146. M. W. Green, "Animal Husbandry at Uruk in the Archaic Period," *Journal of Near Eastern Studies* 39, no. 1 (1980): 5; Krystyna Szarzynska, "Offerings for the Goddess Inana in Archaic Uruk," *Revue d'Assyriologie et d'Archéologie Orientale* 87, no. 1 (1993): 11, table 1: 7a.

147. Krystyna Szarzynska, "Records of Cloths and Garments in Archaic Uruk/Warka," *Altorientalische Forschungen* 15, no. 2 (1988): 228: T-19.

148. Ibid., T-20.

149. Ibid., T-22–23.

150. Ibid., T-18.

151. Ibid., T-20.

152. Ibid., T-21.

153. Ibid., T-29.

154. Ibid., T-38.

155. Ibid., T-6.

156. Ibid., T-12.

157. Ibid., T-10.

158. Ibid., T-11.

159. Denise Schmandt-Besserat, "The Envelopes That Bear the First Writing," *Technology and Culture* 21, no. 3 (1980): 375.

160. René Labat, *Manuel d'épigraphie akkadienne* (Paris: Imprimerie Nationale, 1948), pp. 204–205.

161. Mogens Weitemeyer, *Some Aspects of the Hiring of Workers in the Sippar Region at the Time of Hammurabi* (Copenhagen: Munksgaard International Booksellers and Publishers, 1962), p. 12.

162. W 20987.7: 7 and 20987.27: 3.

163. W 2566, 7176, 8206, 8945, 16235.

164. François Thureau-Dangin, "Notes assyriologiques," *Revue d'Assyriologie et d'Archéologie Orientale* 29, no. 1 (1932): 23.

165. Vaiman, "Protosumerische Schrift," pp. 17–22; Friberg, *Third Millennium Roots*, pp. 10, 20 (referring to the signs as "cups" and "discs"); Nissen, Damerow, and Englund, *Archaic Bookkeeping*, p. 29.

166. Jöran Friberg, "Numbers and Measures in the Earliest Written Records," *Scientific American* 250, no. 2 (1984): 116.

167. Susa: Sb 1938 and 1946; S.ACR.2130.4.

168. Chogha Mish: envelope on exhibition at the Oriental Institute, University of Chicago.

169. Friberg, *Third Millennium Roots*, p. 46.

170. Marvin A. Powell, Jr., "Sumerian Area Measures and the Alleged Decimal Substratum," *Zeitschrift für Assyriologie* 62, no. 3 (1973): 201; John Chadwick, *The Mycenaean World* (Cambridge: Cambridge University Press, 1976), p. 110.

171. Friberg, *Third Millennium Roots*, p. 21; W 21859, UVB 25, pl. 27k.

172. Sb 1940, M 43, p. 92: 555.

173. Sb 1940, M 43, p. 92: 555.

174. Sb 1927, M 43, p. 91: 539, pl. 68.

175. Terence Grieder, "The Interpretation of Ancient Symbols," *American Anthropologist* 77, no. 4 (1975): 849–855.

176. Nissen, Damerow, and Englund, *Archaic Bookkeeping*, pp. 28–29.

177. Jöran Friberg, "Numbers and Measures," p. 111.

178. Ibid., p. 118.

179. ATU 7.

180. M 43: motifs 692, 629, and 633.

181. Dafi 8a, pp. 52–53, fig. 7: 2 and 8.

182. Mark A. Brandes, *Siegelabrollungen aus den archaischen Bauschichten in Uruk-Warka*, Freiburger altorientalische Studien, vol. 3 (Wiesbaden: Franz Steiner Verlag, 1979), p. 39.

183. The same way of impressing cones by the tip practiced on envelope Sb 1927, M 43, pl. 68: 539 is repeated on tablet Sb 6959, M 43, pl. 79: 620.

184. Sb 1940, M 43, p. 92: 555.

185. Interestingly, starting in the Ur III period (during the late third millennium B.C.), some tablets were protected by clay envelopes.

186. A. A. Vaiman, "Formal'nye osobennosti protosumerkish tekstov," *Vestnik Drevnej Istorii* 119, no. 1 (1972): 124–131; M. W. Green, "The Construction and Implementation of the Cuneiform Writing System," *Visible language* 15, no. 4 (1981): 345–372; D. Silvestri, L. Tonelli, and V. Valeri, *Testi e Segni di Uruk IV* (Naples: Istituto Universitario Orientale, Dipartimento di Studi del Mondo Classico e del Mediterraneo Antico, 1985), pp. 34–42.

5. THE EVOLUTION OF SYMBOLS IN PREHISTORY

1. Harold A. Innis, *Empire and Communications* (Oxford: Clarendon Press, 1950), p. 11.

2. Suzanne K. Langer, *Philosophy in a New Key* (Cambridge: Harvard University Press, 1960), pp. 41–43.

3. Jerome S. Bruner, "On Cognitive Growth II," in Jerome S. Bruner

et al., *Studies in Cognitive Growth* (New York: John Wiley and Sons, 1966), p. 47.

4. Ibid., p. 31.

5. B. Vandermeersch, "Ce que révèlent les sépultures moustériennes de Qafzeh en Israël," *Archeologia* 45 (1972): 12.

6. Ralph S. Solecki, *Shanidar* (London: Allen Lane, Penguin Press, 1972), pp. 174–178.

7. Vandermeersch, "Ce que révèlent les sépultures," p. 5.

8. Simon Davis, "Incised Bones from the Mousterian of Kebara Cave (Mount Carmel) and the Aurignacian of Ha-Yonim Cave (Western Galilee), Israel," *Paléorient* 2, no. 1 (1974): 181–182.

9. Among the sites involved are Ksar Akil, Yabrud II, Hayonim, and Abu-Halka: Ofer Bar-Yosef and Anna Belfer-Cohen, "The Early Upper Paleolithic in Levantine Caves," in J. F. Hoffecker and C. A. Wolf, eds., *The Early Upper Paleolithic: Evidence from Europe and the Near East,* BAR International Series 437 (Oxford, 1988), p. 29.

10. Davis, "Incised Bones," pp. 181–182.

11. Loraine Copeland and Francis Hours, "Engraved and Plain Bone Tools from Jiita (Lebanon) and Their Early Kebaran Context," *Proceedings of the Prehistoric Society,* vol. 43 (1977), pp. 295–301.

12. Jacques Tixier, "Poinçon décoré du Paléolithique Supérieur à Ksar'Aqil (Liban)," *Paléorient* 2, no. 1 (1974): 187–192.

13. Ofer Bar-Yosef and N. Goren, "Natufians Remains in Hayonim Cave," *Paléorient* 1 (1973): fig. 8: 16–17.

14. Jean Perrot, "Le Gisement natufien de Mallaha (Eynan), Israel," *L'Anthropologie* 70, nos. 5–6 (1966): fig. 22: 26. An incised bone radius from Kharaneh IV, phase D, may also date from the same period: Mujahed Muheisen, "The Epipalaeolithic Phases of Kharaneh IV," *Colloque International CNRS, Préhistoire du Levant 2* (Lyons, 1988), p. 11, fig. 7.

15. Donald O. Henry, "Preagricultural Sedentism: The Natufian Example," in T. Douglas Price and James A. Brown, eds., *Prehistoric Hunter-Gatherers* (New York: Academic Press, 1985), p. 376.

16. Phillip C. Edwards, "Late Pleistocene Occupation in Wadi al-Hammeh, Jordan Valley," Ph.D. dissertation, University of Sydney, 1987, fig. 4.29: 3–8; Rose L. Solecki, *An Early Village Site at Zawi Chemi Shanidar,* Bibliotheca Mesopotamica, vol. 13 (Malibu, Calif.: Undena Publications, 1981), pp. 43, 48, 50, pl. 8r, fig. 15p.

17. Anna Belfer-Cohen and Ofer Bar-Yosef, "The Aurignacian at Hayonim Cave," *Paléorient* 7, no. 2 (1981): fig. 8.

18. Enver Y. Bostanci, "Researches on the Mediterranean Coast of Anatolia, a New Paleolithic Site at Beldibi near Antalya," *Anatolia* 4 (1959): 140, pl. 11.

19. Enver Y. Bostanci, "Important Artistic Objects from the Beldibi Excavations," *Antropoloji* 1, no. 2 (1964): 25–31.

20. André Leroi-Gourhan, *Préhistoire de l'art occidental* (Paris: Editions Lucien Mazenod, 1971), pp. 119–121.

21. Denis Peyrony, *Eléments de préhistoire* (Ussel: G. Eyboulet et Fils, 1927), p. 54.

22. Alexander Marshack, *The Roots of Civilization* (New York: McGraw-Hill, 1972).

23. Walter J. Ong, *Orality and Literacy* (New York: Methuen, 1982), p. 46.

24. Marshall McLuhan, *Understanding Media* (New York: New American Library, 1964), pp. 81–90.

25. Jacques Cauvin, *Les Premiers Villages de Syrie-Palestine du IXème au VIIème Millénaire avant J. C.,* Collection de la Maison de l'Orient Méditerranéen Ancien no. 4, Série Archéologique 3 (Lyons: Maison de l' Orient, 1978), p. 111; Jacques Cauvin, "Nouvelles fouilles à Mureybet (Syrie) 1971–72, Rapport préliminaire," *Annales Archéologiques Arabes Syriennes* (1972): 110.

26. Robert J. Braidwood, Bruce Howe, Charles A. Reed, "The Iranian Prehistoric Project," *Science* 133, no. 3469 (1961): 2008.

27. Denise Schmandt-Besserat: "The Use of Clay before Pottery in the Zagros," *Expedition* 16, no. 2 (1974): 11–12; "The Earliest Uses of Clay in Syria," *Expedition* 19, no. 3 (1977): 30–31.

28. Charles L. Redman, *The Rise of Civilization* (San Francisco: W. H. Freeman and Company, 1978), p. 163, fig. 5–18: A.

29. Ignace J. Gelb, *A Study of Writing* (Chicago: University of Chicago Press, 1974), p. 65.

30. Cyril S. Smith, "A Matter of Form," *Isis* 76, no. 4 (1985): 586.

31. C. F. Hockett, "The Origin of Speech," *Scientific American* 203 (1960): 90–91.

32. M. Shackley, *Neanderthal Man* (Hamden, Conn.: Archon Books, 1980), p. 113.

6. TOKENS: THE SOCIOECONOMIC IMPLICATIONS

1. Raymond L. Wilder, *Mathematics as a Cultural System* (New York: Pergamon Press, 1981), p. 30.

2. Timothy K. Earle and Jonathon E. Ericson, *Exchange Systems in Prehistory* (New York: Academic Press, 1977), p. 227; Gary A. Wright, *Obsidian Analyses and Prehistoric Near Eastern Trade: 7500 to 3500 B.C.,* Anthropological Papers no. 57 (Ann Arbor: Museum of Anthropology, University of Michigan, 1969), p. 3.

3. Harriet Crawford, "The Mechanics of the Obsidian Trade: A Suggestion," *Antiquity* 2 (1979): 130.

4. Fredrik Barth, *Nomads of South Persia* (Oslo: Oslo University Press, 1961), p. 99; Jack Goody, *The Domestication of the Savage Mind* (Cambridge: Cambridge University Press, 1978), p. 15.

5. Alexander Marshack, *The Roots of Civilization* (New York: McGraw-Hill, 1972).

6. Jacques Cauvin, *Les Premiers Villages de Syrie-Palestine du IXème au*

VIIème Millénaire Avant J. C., Collection de la Maison de l'Orient Méditer-ranéen Ancien no. 4, Série Archéologique 3 (Lyons: Maison de l'Orient, 1978), p. 74.

7. Robert J. Braidwood, "Seeking the World's First Farmers in Persian Kurdistan," *Illustrated London News,* October 22, 1960, p. 695; Philip E. L. Smith, "Prehistoric Excavations at Ganj Dareh Tepe in 1967," *Vth International Congress of Iranian Art and Archaeology* (Tehran, 1968), p. 187.

8. Cauvin, *Les Premiers Villages,* pp. 40, 41–42; Henri de Contenson, "Tell Aswad (Damascène)," *Paléorient* 5 (1979): 153–154.

9. Smith, "Prehistoric Excavations," p. 186; James Mellaart, *Çatal Hüyük* (New York: McGraw-Hill, 1967).

10. Dietrich Sürenhagen (see vol. 1, BW, p. 67, fig. 34).

11. Hans J. Nissen, "The Archaic Texts from Uruk," *World Archaeology* 17, no. 3 (1986): 326.

12. Claude Meillassoux, "On the Mode of Production of the Hunting Band," in Pierre Alexandre, ed., *French Perspectives in African Studies* (London: Oxford University Press, 1973), pp. 189, 194.

13. Mark Nathan Cohen, "Prehistoric Hunter-Gatherers: The Meaning of Social Complexity," in T. Douglas Price and James A. Brown, eds., *Prehistoric Hunter-Gatherers* (New York: Academic Press, 1985), p. 99. Meillassoux, "On the Mode of Production," p. 194.

14. Morton H. Fried, *The Evolution of Political Society: An Essay in Political Anthropology* (New York: Random House, 1967), p. 109.

15. Cohen, "Prehistoric Hunter-Gathers," p. 105.

16. Charles L. Redman, *The Rise of Civilization* (San Francisco: W. H. Freeman and Company, 1978), p. 203.

17. Cauvin, *Les Premiers Villages,* p. 43.

18. Olivier Aurenche, "Chronologie et organisation de l'espace dans le Proche Orient," *Prehistoire du Levant,* Colloque CNRS no. 598 (Lyons, 1980), pp. 1–11.

19. Arthur J. Tobler, *Excavations at Tepe Gawra,* vol. 2, University Museum Monographs (Philadelphia: University of Pennsylvania, 1950), p. 60.

20. Redman, *Rise of Civilization,* p. 197.

21. Marcia Ascher and Robert Ascher, *Code of the Quipu* (Ann Arbor: University of Michigan Press, 1981), p. 63.

22. Yvonne Rosengarten, *Le Concept sumérien de consommation dans la vie économique et religieuse* (Paris: Editions E. de Boccard, 1960).

23. Tohru Maeda, "On the Agricultural Festivals in Sumer," *Acta Sumerologica* 5, no. 1 (1979): 24–25; Rosengarten, *Le Concept sumérien,* p. 255.

24. Albert A. Trouworst, "From Tribute to Taxation: On the Dynamics of the Early State," in Henri J. M. Claessen and Pieter van de Velde, eds., *Early State Dynamics* (Leiden: E. J. Brill, 1987), p. 133.

25. Pierre Amiet, *La Glyptique mésopotamienne archaïque* (Paris: Editions du CNRS, 1980), p. 434, pl. 46: 656; p. 499, pl. 120: 1606–1607, 1609.

26. Mark A. Brandes, *Siegelabrollungen aus den archaischen Bauschichten*

in Uruk-Warka, Freiburger altorientalische Studien, vol. 3 (Wiesbaden: Franz Steiner Verlag, 1979), pt. 2, pls. 1–11.

27. Enrica Fiandra, "The Connection between Clay Sealings and Tablets in Administration," *South Asian Archaeology* (1979): 36–38.

28. Marvin A. Powell, Jr., "Sumerian Numeration and Metrology," Ph.D. dissertation, University of Minnesota, 1971, p. 208.

29. Thomas W. Beale, "Beveled Rim Bowls and Their Implications for Change and Economic Organization in the Later Fourth Millennium B.C.," *Journal of Near Eastern Studies* 37, no. 4 (1978): 291–292.

30. UVB 2, figs. 16–17; Henri de Genouillac, *Fouilles de Telloh,* vol. 1, *Epoques présargoniques* (Paris: Paul Geuthner, 1934), p. 64; M 46, p. 151 and pl. 89; P. Delougaz and Helene J. Kantor, "New Evidence for the Prehistoric and Protoliterate Culture Development of Khuzestan," *The Memorial Volume of the Vth International Congress of Iranian Art and Archaeology,* vol. 1 (Tehran, 1972), p. 27; André Finet, "Bilan provisoire des fouilles belges du Tell Kannas," *Annual of the American Schools of Oriental Research* 44 (1979): 93.

7. COUNTING AND THE EMERGENCE OF WRITING

1. Leslie A. White, *The Science of Culture* (New York: Grove Press, 1949), p. 286.

2. Raymond L. Wilder, *Evolution of Mathematical Concepts* (New York: John Wiley and Sons, 1968), p. 180.

3. Bertrand Russell, *Introduction to Mathematical Philosophy* (London: George Allen and Unwin, 1960), p. 3.

4. Tobias Danzig, *Number: The Language of Science,* 4th ed. (New York: Macmillan, 1959), p. 6; Graham Flegg, *Numbers, Their History and Meaning* (New York: Schocken Books, 1983), pp. 8–14; Edna E. Kramer, *The Nature and Growth of Modern Mathematics* (New York: Hawthorn Books, 1970), pp. 4–5; David E. Smith, *History of Mathematics,* vol. 1 (Boston: Ginn and Company, 1951), pp. 6–8.

5. Levi Leonard Conant, *The Number Concept* (London: Macmillan, 1896), p. 28; Arthur Chervin, *Anthropologie bolivienne* (Paris: Librairie H. Le Soudier, 1908), p. 229; Georges Ifrah, *From One to Zero* (New York: Viking Penguin, 1985), p. 7; Smith, *History of Mathematics,* p. 6.

6. Karl Menninger, *Number Words and Number Symbols,* rev. ed. (Cambridge: MIT Press, 1977), p. 33.

7. Aletta Biersack, "The Logic of Misplaced Concreteness: Paiela Body Counting and the Nature of the Primitive Mind," *American Anthropologist* 84, no. 4 (1982): 813.

8. Franz Boas, "Fifth Report on the Northwestern Tribes of Canada," *Proceedings of the British Association for the Advancement of Science* (1889): 881.

9. Igor M. Diakonoff, "Some Reflections on Numerals in Sumerian

towards a History of Mathematical Speculations," *Journal of the American Oriental Society* 103, no. 1 (1983): 88.

10. Jack Goody, *The Domestication of the Savage Mind* (Cambridge: Cambridge University Press, 1977), p. 13.

11. Diakonoff, "Some Reflections," p. 92.

12. Marvin A. Powell, Jr., "Sumerian Numeration and Metrology," Ph.D. dissertation, University of Minnesota, 1971, pp. 27–28.

13. François Thureau-Dangin, "Le Système ternaire dans la numération sumérienne," *Revue d'Assyriologie et d'Archéologie Orientale* 25, no. 2 (1928): 119–121.

14. Diakonoff, "Some Reflections," p. 90.

15. Powell, "Sumerian Numeration," p.30.

16. Powell notes that "diš" is attested for counting plots of lands. Ibid., p. 18.

17. Ibid., p. 13.

18. Ibid., pp. 23, 28–29, 14.

19. Diakonoff, "Some Reflections," pp. 84–87, 88.

20. A. A. Vaiman, "Die Bezeichnung von Sklaven und Sklavinnen in der protosumerischen Schrift," BaM 20 (1989): 126–127; A. A. Vaiman, "Über die Protosumerische Schrift," *Acta Antiqua Academiae Scientiarum Hungaricae* 22 (1974): 20–23.

21. Peter Damerow and Robert K. Englund, "Die Zahlzeichensysteme der archaischen Texte aus Uruk," ZATU 165; Hans J. Nissen, Peter Damerow, and Robert K. Englund, *Archaic Bookkeeping* (Chicago: University of Chicago Press, 1994), pp. 25–29.

22. Jöran Friberg, *The Third Millennium Roots of Babylonian Mathematics. 1. A Method for Decipherment, through Mathematical and Metrological Analysis, of Proto-Sumerian and Proto-Elamite Semi-pictographic Inscriptions* (Göteborg: Chalmers University of Technology and University of Göteborg, 1978–1979), pp. 10, 15, 21, 46.

23. Alexander Marshack, *The Roots of Civilization* (New York: McGraw-Hill, 1972).

24. There can be no doubt about the distinction between these two subtypes, since large as well as small tetrahedrons are both included in the same envelope from Susa: Sb 1967. In fact, Sb 1967 yields tetrahedrons of three subtypes: small, large, and punctated.

25. Dafi 8a, pp. 32–34.

26. Stephen J. Lieberman, "Of Clay Pebbles, Hollow Clay Balls and Writing: A Sumerian View," *American Journal of Archaeology* 184, no. 3 (1980): 339–358.

27. Pierre Amiet, *L'Age des échanges inter-iraniens* (Paris: Editions de la Réunion des Musées Nationaux, 1986), p. 87.

28. Jöran Friberg, "Preliterate Counting and Accounting in the Middle East," *Orientalistische Literaturzeitung* 89, nos. 5–6 (1994): 484; G. van Driel, "Tablets from Jebel Aruda," in G. van Driel, Th. J. H. Krispijn,

M. Stol, and K. R. Veenhof, eds., *Zikir Šumim,* Assyriological Studies Presented to F. R. Kraus on the Occasion of His Seventieth Birthday (Leiden: E. J. Brill, 1982), p. 14: 6, 2, and 7.

29. Jöran Friberg, "Numbers and Measures in the Earliest Written Records," *Scientific American* 250, no. 2 (1984): 116.

30. François Thureau-Dangin, *Esquisse d'une histoire du système sexagesimal* (Paris: Librairie Orientaliste Paul Geuthner, 1932), pp. 6–7.

31. David E. Smith, *Number and Numerals* (New York: Bureau of Publications, Teachers College, Columbia University, 1937), p. 8.

32. Ignace J. Gelb, *A Study of Writing,* rev. ed. (Chicago: University of Chicago Press, 1974), p. 67.

8. CONCLUSIONS

1. Georges Charbonnier, *Conversations with Claude Lévi-Strauss* (London: Cape Editions, 1973), pp. 27–28.

Glossary

Because the topic of tokens is new, the existing vocabulary is often inadequate. I note here the meaning I give to some of the key words used in the text.

Bulla: Oblong or biconoid clay tag bearing seals. I propose that some of these artifacts secured strings of tokens (figs. 10 and 11).

Complex token: Token typical of the fourth-millennium B.C. temple administration. This category includes all sixteen types of tokens described above. The artifacts are characterized by an extensive use of markings, either linear, punctated, or appliqué (figs. 5 and 6).

Counter: Because the function of tokens was counting and accounting, I use "token" and "counter" as synonyms.

Docket: An object testifying for an amount of labor done and meant to be exchanged for a payment.

Envelope: Hollow clay ball of spherical, ovoid, or oblong shape holding tokens and usually bearing seal impressions (figs. 12 and 13).

Impressed tablet: Tablet bearing notations impressed by tokens or by the blunt end of a stylus. These tablets used to be referred to in the literature as "numerical tablets." I argue that the signs refer not to numbers but to units of goods (fig. 18).

Incised tablet: Tablet bearing signs traced with the sharp end of a stylus (fig. 25).

Marking: A protoliterate sign which is a forerunner of writing (figs. 15, 16, and 18).

Near East: Synonymous with "Middle East." It includes the following countries: Iran, Iraq, Turkey, Syria, Lebanon, Jordan, and Israel or the ancient provinces of Persia, Mesopotamia, Anatolia, Syria, and Palestine.

Pictographic tablet: Tablet bearing signs traced with the sharp end of a stylus. Formerly, "pictographic" meant "picture writing" in the sense that the signs were in the shape of the things they represented. In this book, "pictographic" also refers to signs that perpetuate the shape of tokens (fig. 25).

Plain token: Token typical of the periods between 8000 and 4300 B.C. and after 3100 B.C. The shapes are mostly restricted to cones, spheres, disks, cylinders, and tetrahedrons. The surface is usually plain (fig. 3).

Sign: A written character (fig. 25).

Token: Small artifact, generally modeled in clay according to one of the following sixteen types: cones, spheres, disks, cylinders, tetrahedrons, ovoids, quadrangles, triangles, biconoids, paraboloids, bent coils, ovals/rhomboids, vessels, tools, animals, and miscellaneous. I propose that these objects were used as counters to keep records of goods (fig. 4).

Index

1371